$2.00

CAPTAIN DUNCAN MACLAIN, *famous blind sleuth, and his Seeing Eye dogs are back again in Baynard Kendrick's most difficult, puzzling murder.*

DEATH KNELL

By BAYNARD KENDRICK

Author of *Blind Man's Bluff,* etc.

Everything was going smoothly at the Jordans' cocktail party. Mingled chatter and care-free laughter rose in telegraphic waves to Duncan Maclain, sitting quietly on the sofa, his Seeing Eye dog at his knee. And then gorgeous Troy Singleton appeared, bringing a pause that definitely was *not* refreshing. . . .

From that moment on events tumbled pell-mell toward a tragedy that nearly

(continued on back flap)

This book has appeared serially under the title *Private Investigator Maclain.*

A MORROW MYSTERY

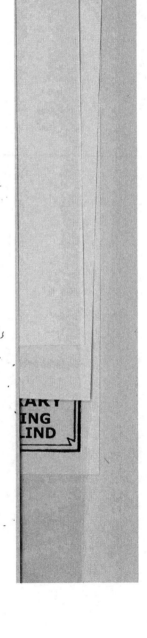

157   20.

DEATH
KNELL

Books by Baynard Kendrick:

BLOOD ON LAKE LOUISA

THE IRON SPIDERS

THE ELEVEN OF DIAMONDS

THE LAST EXPRESS*

THE WHISTLING HANGMAN*

DEATH BEYOND THE GO-THRU

THE ODOR OF VIOLETS*

BLIND MAN'S BLUFF*

DEATH KNELL*

* A Duncan Maclain Mystery.

BAYNARD KENDRICK

DEATH KNELL

A
DUNCAN MACLAIN
MYSTERY

BOOKS INC. *distributed by*
WILLIAM MORROW & COMPANY
NEW YORK : 1945

This book has appeared serially under the title
Private Investigator Maclain

PRINTED IN THE UNITED STATES OF AMERICA

To

Sgt. Baynard Kendrick, Jr.

United States Marine Corps

. . . —

CONTENTS

DEATH
KNELL

"If it be now, . . . "

I

Larmar Jordan's study on the fourteenth floor of the Arday Apartments at Tenth Street and Fifth Avenue had been pictured in *House Beautiful*. Its thirty-foot expanse flowed out through modern French doors to combine smoothly with a red flagstoned terrace, bright now with four umbrella-topped tables. A striped awning strung across the east end formed a sheltering bower encircled on three sides with green-boxed hedges, where five days a week, weather permitting, Larmar Jordan sat at his desk from two until six intent on the composition of novels which had brought him fame. (*Queen's Gambit*, 1932; *Richmond*, 1934; and topping a string of others the latest *Monsignor's Wife*, 1943.)

A cocktail party was in session.

Comfortable in the embrace of a wide divan just inside the doors one of the guests, Captain Duncan Maclain, set an empty cocktail glass on the end table beside him and fell into the delightful pastime of cataloguing those present through the medium of sound.

The Captain was blind, had been for more than twenty years, yet reinforced with a streak of iron persistence, and urged on by his closest friend, Spud Savage, he had dismissed hopelessness as the refuge of a weakling. Searching for a difficult task to master, something which might restore waning confidence in himself, he had drawn on his experience as an ex-intelligence officer and turned to the most unlikely of all pursuits for a blind

I

man—that of a private investigator. That he was still alive after
many years of such a profession spoke less of his almost fool-
hardy inclination to take chances than of the meticulous nicety
with which he had mastered the demanding details of such a
hazardous career.

He had been shot three times, but endless hours of rigorous
training in firing at sound had made him an even more deadly
shot in return. Well past forty, he still moved with the ease and
sureness of a body in perfect trim, following his Seeing Eye dog,
Schnucke, at a pace much faster than the normal walk of a
man who could see.

A woman in a light gray sports suit swung in from the terrace
with a long manly stride, stared at Maclain's well-marked jaw,
mobile face, and crisp dark hair, and after a moment sat down
beside him.

"I'm Sarah Hanley, Larmar's agent. Aren't you being neg-
lected, Captain Maclain?"

"If I am, it's my own fault, Miss Hanley. I sneaked in here to
get Schnucke away from the crowd on the terrace. People per-
sist in feeding her canapes. She's weak—"

"But beautiful." Sarah Hanley glanced down at the German
shepherd lying close to the Captain's feet. Schnucke acknowledged the attention with a delicate yawn. Sarah Hanley moved
her slightly protuberant brown eyes back to Maclain. "I'm really
Mrs. Hanley—outside of the office, of course. You're engaged to
Sybella Ford, aren't you?"

She gave him scarcely a chance to nod before plunging on.
"She's charming. So clever! I never understood how anyone
could tell good antiques from fakes. I have terrible taste, really.
Imagine making a success of an antique shop—or decorating
anyone's home."

"You seem to have made a success of picking good writers," remarked Maclain.

"But that's different." She laughed, throatily. "One just picks what one likes to read, then it's in the lap of the gods. Now I've always thought you could do a wonderful book, Captain Maclain—".

Somewhere in the apartment a musical doorbell rang with a double chime.

Blindness had endowed the Captain with an ability to listen in apparent rapt attention to a speaker while following many happenings which swirled about him on concurrent waves of sound.

Out on the terrace Sybella was chatting with Paul Hirst, Larmar's secretary. Cocktails raised her voice a trifle, but it never annoyed Maclain who loved the friendly laughter of her tone. Hirst was a small precise man—not over five foot two, Maclain had judged from walking beside him. Like so many men short of stature his voice was booming and full. Mingled with Sybella's humorous lilt it drifted in through a babel of clinking glasses, and babbling conversation.

Authors talking shop, a little drunk: "Whassamatter paper? Take some they're wrapping up all the parcels in. Use sommait! Tha's whassamatter. Use—"

"Spend sumpin on a'vetizzin. I tol' him."

"Now look—"

Loud voices; soft voices; deep voices; voices high and thin. A woman's voice being sweetly catty—"She's lovely, of course— or should I say *but coarse?*"—not realizing how whispers often filter in.

Sarah Hanley was growing enthusiastic. "—now just take some of your adventures as a detective, Captain Maclain. All you'd need to do is put them down. I mean simply write them *down*. It would—"

Soft footsteps crossed the study. The Captain recognized the trained even stride of Harry, the Jordans' Negro houseman. He even sorted out from Sarah Hanley's gushing the pause of indecision as Harry opened the door.

"How do you do, Miss Singleton." There might have been surprise, even fear in the houseman's greeting. Certainly the Captain read puzzlement there, if no more—a break in the normal routine of a well-coached servant—the irresolute pause which might indicate anyone from a policeman to a bill collector at the door.

"Hello, Harry!" There was no indecision on the part of the woman who came in unless it was a tiny edge of truculence, well covered by the pleasant timbre of her greeting. "Schooled," the Captain thought. "A superb actress who has learned how to speak without offending the ear. If she let herself go she'd be shrill."

Miss Singleton sailed across the study leaving a trailing breath of fine perfume. She tossed a "Sarah, *darling!*" toward Maclain's companion, who broke her literary advice with a startled, "Oh!"

Suddenly the chatter on the terrace was very still to burst again with a redoubled vigor.

"You were saying—" prompted Maclain.

"Larmar's a god damn fool," Sarah Hanley announced with feeling. "I wonder if he really asked Troy Singleton here, or if she had the guts to just bust in!" She stood up and added abstractedly, "You'll think about the book, Captain. It's time for me to go home."

Schnucke stirred uneasily and got up, moving close to the Captain's knee in a stance of quiet defiance. A patter of paws crossed the chenille rug and dubiously hesitated a short distance away. Schnucke pressed closer with a muffled growl.

"You're a nasty old witch," Maclain told his dog good-humoredly. "That's Winnie, the Jordan's cocker. He's tried to make friends every time you've been here. Now be polite and lie down."

She obeyed grudgingly. Maclain snapped his fingers and patted the sofa. Winnie jumped up and settled close beside him while the Captain scratched first one silky long ear and then the other.

Harry came by and gave the Captain another cocktail.

A man came in from the terrace, stepping cautiously across the sill.

"It that your dog?"

"Which one?" The Captain smiled.

"The big one. I know Winnie. He's staring at her with a lovelorn frown."

"Yes, she's mine."

"Hell, you're Duncan Maclain. I should have known. I'm slightly oiled. I'm Bob Morse of the *Globe-Tribune*. Do you mind if I sit down?"

"Not at all."

The divan sagged. Morse smelled of good tobacco, and soap and water, overlaid with an effluvium of expensive imported gin. "Hell. I've got to quit drinking. I'm getting as fat as Boule-de-suif the de Maupassant butter-ball. If I gain any more they'll ration me." He sighed with an intoxicating exhalation. "I saw you talking with Hanley."

"Umm." Maclain sipped his Martini.

"Leave it to that old bag to back a blind man up against the wall. I'm sorry—"

"Forget it." The Captain grinned. "Haven't you written for the *New Yorker?*"

"Profiles." Morse chuckled. "Good God! Have I broken out into Braille?"

"Not exactly. My secretary reads off records for me if she happens to run across something of interest. She picked on yours about the Washington tailor."

"I'll invite myself up to hear it sometime. Morse on wax. I'm doing one on Larmar now." He paused to swallow. "What did Horse-face Hanley say about the arrival of Helen of Troy?"

"She seemed upset," Maclain said warily. "If you mean Miss Singleton."

"That's who I mean." Morse smacked his lips. "It's a pity you can't see her—something for the book is little Troy. It would certainly hop up my profile if I could tell the truth about Troy. There's one baby who won't be a cinnamon bun to have all the raisins picked out by baker-boy Larmar—"

The Captain touched his Braille watch. "You'll have to excuse me, Mr. Morse."

"Excuse *me.*" Morse's voice was quiet and more steady. "I'm a pig when I get mad and when I get drunk I get mad. I hope you haven't got me wrong. How well do you know Larmar?"

"I've been here several times," said Duncan Maclain.

"Then you know Lucia."

"She's charming."

"That's what I think." Morse stood up and placed a pudgy hand on the Captain's shoulder bearing him down. "Still and all, I like Larmar. Now the whole damn town knows that he and Lucia don't get along. Maybe she's too good a wife for him. Maybe—hell, I don't know and I'm trying to write about him. All I know is it isn't kosher to give a cocktail party in your home and trot in mistress number thirteen—or is it twenty-four?"

A couple of guests were departing, throwing laughing good-bys toward Morse and the Captain. Someone clapped Morse on the shoulder, but he didn't turn around. His pudgy hand grew heavier, weighing the Captain down. With drunken persistence he went steadily on, breathing fumes of alcohol, building up a latent idea.

"Sadishm's the word for it, Cap'n Maclain." Morse's speech had thickened as the last cocktail went down. "Larmar hates Lucia. Wants to hurt her all the time. Likes to hurt her—s'why he brings Troy here. Likes to hurt all women. See the booksh he reads sometime. See him sittin' at deshk out there now. Where's Lucia? Inna houshe—tha's where. Gone inna housh to cry."

He was seized with a touch of drunken tears. " 'Member what Shakespeare saysh, Cap'n M'lain—good ole Shakespeare— never wrong—'if it be not now, yet it will come!' "

"What will come?" asked Duncan Maclain.

" 'Sdeath!" Morse let go a wave of alcoholic fumes in one mysterious whisper. The weight on the Captain's shoulder was gratifyingly relaxed. Morse waddled unsteadily toward the hall.

Winnie, the cocker, lay asleep pressed close to the Captain's leg, luxuriating in the softness of the sofa's forbidden down.

Bob Morse had left a disturbing thought from *Hamlet* that kept marching funereally through the Captain's agile brain.

"If it be now, 'tis not to come; if it be not to come, it will be now; if it be not now, yet it will come: the readiness is all."

Repeating it he found himself left with a depressing sense of being ineffectual. Elements of love and jealousy had played about him at a cocktail party and woven themselves into an ugly pattern. Hate and unhappiness were storing up energy which might strike and shatter from the heart of a storm.

" 'Sdeath!" Morse had whispered. The newspaper man was drunk, but he wasn't a fool. Maclain felt as hopeless as a minister trying to stop a war. "If it be not to come, it will be now!"

With a sudden crash of sound the carillon in the steeple of the church across Fifth Avenue started its clanging song. It was startlingly near—booming out the notes of *Adeste Fidelis* with a vibration that leaped across the terrace and seemed to fill the room. Maclain touched the sofa beside him and found that Winnie had gone.

Sybella came in and said above the din, "The chimes mean it's nearly six. They play every afternoon." The Captain nodded and reached to take her hand. She smiled and went on, "I looked in a couple of times and you seemed quite happy in your nest of dogs, so I let you alone. What have you been doing for amusement outside of knocking yourself out with gin?"

"Listening to our hostess weeping," said Duncan Maclain. "She's somewhere behind me in another room."

2

Success had armored Larmar Jordan with an infolding layer of insolence which hid the truth that underneath he was really re-tiring, to a point of being shy.

Seated at his desk on the terrace, with the cocktail party in full swing, he allowed his guests to seek him out rather than disturb himself with the more gracious effort of mingling among them. Supplicants for his attention were accorded skillfully graded greetings which ranged from the briefest of handclasps and most fleeting of smiles to several minutes of scintillating con-

versation dished up in Larmar's headiest style. The exact grada-
tion stemmed from the donor's almost psychic knowledge of
what people could best help the career of author Larmar.

There was one guest whom Larmar found most difficult to
classify, the blind Capt. Duncan Maclain. The Captain was always polite, even heartily appreciative of *Monsignor's Wife,*
which he had read in Braille. Yet back of Maclain's courteous
acceptance of friendship and hospitality Larmar sensed a thread
of tolerance manifested by a reticence hard to define.

Over a period of months Duncan Maclain's aloofness had become a challenge to the efficacy of Larmar Jordan's charm. It
was disconcerting to like a man who couldn't see the tasteful cut
of your clothes, the humorous twinkle in your eyes, or the warmth
of your grin. The visual lack of gestures made fiction cold. Larmar could write, but he wondered how one impressed a man who
judged each speech by the character of its sound.

He watched the Captain and Schnucke leave the terrace and
take a seat inside the door. After a moment Sarah Hanley
ducked in and joined him. "She'll get short shrift," thought
Larmar. There was some consolation in the idea that Maclain
was aloof with others too.

"As I said before, you have the technique. It's the technique
and not the content that makes your books sell—"

A girl, whose name Larmar didn't know, was perched on the
desk beside him clutching a cocktail glass in her hand. She had
deep brown eyes which burned with fanatical fervor. Oblivious
to the other guests, she was vehemently attempting to change
Jordan's character by pouring a ten-minute cascade of words into
his non-receptive ear.

"I'm glad I have something." Larmar slid his long slender
body more languidly down in the chair. "Are you a critic?"

"The world is your critic, Larmar." She edged closer, almost brushing him with one rayon covered knee.

"Indeed?" His pale blue eyes followed the line of her thin green dress where the desk drew it tight over hip and thigh. She was young, but youth scarcely gave her the privilege of reading his books and immediately calling him Larmar.

"You have no consciousness of change—no realization of conflict," she galloped on. "Your women are weak creatures of the flesh. They live in the past, blind to the conflict of Negro and white, of capital and labor, of Gentile and Jew. They know only the conflict of the sexes—"

"You've used the word 'conflict' three times, darling." Larmar reached out and patted her leg above the knee. "Is it something new?"

A young man, sparkling white in the ducks of a Lieutenant, j.g. bustled up. "Kit! I've looked all over for you."

"She's been right here, Lieutenant." Larmar removed his hand with commendable promptness. "Kit doesn't like my women."

"But apparently you do." The young officer consulted his wrist watch, then fixed unfriendly eyes on a point slightly above Larmar's wavy yellow hair. "We have a dinner engagement. You'll pardon us, I'm sure."

Kit slid from the desk and trotted off after him. Larmar watched them leave the terrace.

"Boorish, isn't he?"

He turned slowly to face Lucia at the other end of the desk. Her ingenuous blue eyes were bright with a malicious twinkle.

"A friend of yours, isn't he, darling?" Larmar's irregular white teeth showed in an annoying semblance of a smile.

"I thought you might find Kit amusing." Lucia smoothed her

tailored cocktail slacks, touched her ash blond hair and turned half away to nod to someone across the terrace. "She's just a child."

"Overactive glands, perhaps," said Larmar nastily. "She seemed quite well developed to me. If you're deliberately trying to get me involved with someone else, Lucia, pick out one who doesn't use a T-square to cut her hair."

"Aren't you involved enough already, darling?"

He stood up slowly. She could irritate him more thoroughly than anyone living, and his face and tone were ugly when he asked her, "What do you mean?"

"Isn't that Troy Singleton that Harry just let in?" She watched him pale and redden, then added, "I'm sure she won't be guarded by an officer who might create a scene."

"If she's here, you asked her." His voice spoke honest disbelief as he stared at the trim black-haired figure framed in the study door.

Lucia said mockingly, "Now, really, dear. This seems to be the point where the wife goes to her room."

The terrace was quiet for a space of three quick steps as Lucia walked away. Larmar picked up an empty cocktail glass from the desk and replaced it, then reached a sudden decision, skirted two tables doubly noisy with the chatter of guests nervous with pointed unconcern. At the study door he stretched out both hands and took Troy Singleton's firmly in his own.

"This is delightful, Troy." If he was seething inside he cleverly failed to show it. An airy wave of a hand took in the terrace. "You know everyone, I believe." Before she could answer, he had led her to the desk and installed her, back to the crowd, in the place occupied a few minutes before by the garrulous Kit.

Harry came with cocktails.

Over the glass furious black eyes, made more striking by tiny red glints of rage, opened wide and silently cursed Larmar.

"What makes you think I know everyone?"

"Don't you?" He took an innocent interest in the olive at the bottom of his glass. "I thought you'd met most of them."

"Where would I meet them?"

"Oh, around town."

"Around town," she mimicked. Her fingers closed tightly on the glass stem threatening to break it. They were well shaped fingers, tapered and strong with oval nails done in a polish of reddish brown. A large square diamond on her right hand burned in the rays of the lowering sun.

"You know Bob Morse."

"Naturally. Every girl who's checked hats in a night club knows that drunken bum." She gulped her drink. Lipstick showed on the rim. "I thought when you asked me here this afternoon that you wanted me to meet people. I wouldn't have come—not to be herded to your desk like a farmer stabling a cow."

Larmar's pale blue eyes crinkled at the corners. He put up a hand to shield them. The crowd on the terrace was thinning already, couples drifting with obvious nonchalance toward the study to scuttle gratefully through the door.

He moved his gaze to Troy, thinking idly how perfect she was in face and figure, too perfect, perhaps, to be quite real—a sight to arouse men's emotions like the picture of a Varga girl.

"You're very far from being a cow, darling," he said. "The only trouble is I *didn't* ask you to come."

"Really?" Troy cupped her round chin in one hand and rested

her elbow on her knee. "I'll forgive you because you're tight, Larmar."

He regarded her in silence and decided after a time that she was serious. "What makes you think I'm tight, darling?"

"Aren't you?"

"I've had two cocktails—no more."

"You'd have to be drunk to deliberately lie to me."

"Yes," he admitted, his eyes half puzzled. "Yes, I would. Decidedly."

"Then why did you say you never invited me? Is it some new form of humiliation?"

"It's the truth," declared Larmar.

Troy straightened up and took a half sheet of notepaper from an initialed bag that hung pendent from her slender shoulder. She held it out wordlessly.

Larmar read it, refolded the two sharp creases and put it in his pocket.

"I want that back, please," said Troy.

"I'll return it when I find out who wrote it," he told her. He was looking across the terrace toward the French windows that led to Lucia's bedroom.

"It's written on your paper—"

"And typewriter," he finished for her. "Still I didn't write it, Troy." He turned back to face her, speaking earnestly. "Do you think I'd be so foolish as to ask you up here?"

"Why not?" She was dangerously angry again.

"Because I think too much of you to subject you to insults—particularly in my own home. It's not your fault or mine, Troy. It's just one of those impossible situations that both of us know."

She bit one full lip into a deeper crimson. "And now that I'm here in answer to this mysterious invitation, are you going to introduce me to anyone?"

"Certainly," he told her quietly, "anyone you want to know. Can you take it?"

"No!" She slid down from the desk. "But, I can take a hint if it's tossed at me with both fists, Larmar." She gave an ugly little laugh. "Some day you may meet a situation you can't quite handle. I hope I'm there."

"I hope so too, darling. I enjoy your company."

"I'm relieving you of it right now. Don't bother to rise. It will attract too much attention. Harry will see me out." She marched across the terrace.

Larmar waited until she was gone, then sauntered over and stepped through the windows into Lucia's room.

His wife was stretched out on a blue chaise longue trailing a current issue of *Good Housekeeping* on the floor beside her. She raised it at the sound of Larmar's step and began to study an illustration with marked overinterest. He kicked a chintz-covered puff up close beside her and sat down.

"Guests all gone?" Lucia asked the question without relaxing her smug perusal of the magazine.

"I'm sure I don't know," said Larmar stolidly. "And furthermore I don't give a tinker's damn. They came here at your invitation—not mine."

"All of them?" Lucia lowered the magazine.

"All of them," he told her firmly. "You're not very clever, Lucia. In fact, when you get jealous, you're quite obvious." He took the note from his pocket and tossed it in her lap. "What the hell was the idea of sending this to Troy Singleton? What did you think you'd gain by standing this cocktail party on its ear?"

"Larmy, what's the use?" The note lay untouched. Lucia used

the affectionate contraction of his name which he hadn't heard in a year. Her voice was very weary, her expressive face very pale. "We're getting nowhere fast. You're seen all over New York with the Singleton girl. I've kept my mouth shut, but it hurts when you take me for a fool and try to contrive some silly trick to foist the blame on me for bringing her here."

He stood up, cold and unresponsive. Lucia's fingers closed tightly on the magazine as though she might rip it in two, then letting it slip to the floor she began to cry.

"God, what an actress!" said Larmar, staring with a frown. "Make it loud, darling. Plenty of good throaty sobs so that the whole house can't help hearing you!"

Across the street the bells in the steeple started their afternoon song. Lucia's sobs grew louder.

"Even Maclain in the study can't hear you now, darling." Larmar grinned. "Those damn chimes will ring for fifteen minutes. I wonder if you can hold out that long!"

3

It had always been a secret irritation to Paul Hirst that his employer chose to regard him in the light of a very efficient machine. As a matter of fact, life itself never resembled any deep flowing river to Paul. It rushed along rapidly, its swift shallow current broken by myriad sharp stones of petty irritations.

Paul fought his progress vigorously, like a skillful paddler shooting the rapids in a birch bark canoe. Some day, he feared his hand might slip and he would find himself boatless and struggling helplessly in the middle of anger's frothy stream. The sharp jagged rock which he feared the most and which presented itself recurrently, at every turn, was his employer, Larmar.

He didn't resent Jordan's position, for the author's success added greatly to his own. But, he chafed at the spacious hand with which God had dealt bodily gifts to Larmar. Larmar was tall, expansive, casual with his women, and addicted to loose expensive clothes, which hung on his long, lithe frame as though they had finally found a home of their own.

Paul was short. He bought expensive clothes himself, but no matter how well they were tailored, they always felt too small. In talking to Larmar, Paul always had a sensation of bending his neck back. It made him feel like a puppy dog asking largess from a king on an inaccessible throne.

Actually, he was quite a decent little fellow, a trifle conceited, with a brain as sharp as they come. It was unfortunate, perhaps, that circumstances and his own capability brought him to work with Larmar. There was too much propinquity with a man too tall. To bolster his morale, Paul had adopted the truculence of a lion in bantam rooster's clothing. This he liked to turn loose acidulously on those unfortunate enough to cross his path outside of the Jordans' home.

He liked his work, but he hated Larmar's parties. They were added hazards to life's turbulent course, almost waterfalls threatening to wreck his canoe. Larmar, whose ingrained streak of sadism occasionally showed up grinning with skeleton teeth, took a delight in never having made Paul Hirst's social position quite clear. Paul was supposed to attend, but he was equally supposed to use a nicely balanced amount of judicious self effacement. Certain guests he might talk to, others he was expected to let severely alone. Finding the dividing line kept him hopping about with the agility of an epileptic flea.

The cocktail party was no exception. He had been doubly sandpapered by the arrival of Troy. He disapproved heartily of Larmar's philandering. There had been others, varying in degree.

Paul liked Lucia, who was considerate of his standing in the household in her nonchalant way. Yet watching his employer over a period of years, he was still undecided as to how much any one woman meant to Larmar. He had never discovered any deep involvement, unless perhaps, it was Troy. Rather, they seemed to come and go with the rapidity of tiny clouds dancing across the face of the sun.

Troy, Paul believed, was the cleverest of the lot, but even she had slipped. Paul felt instinctively that her ill-timed arrival at the Jordan party would be the end of Troy.

To add to his pique, Larmar had disappeared into Lucia's bedroom and left the onus of speedily deserting guests to Paul. Somehow, under a cloak of well concealed embarrassment, he finally got rid of them all.

He went out and indulged himself in a good dinner at a near-by cafe, but it failed to relax him. Larmar's handwritten manuscript had to be typed before morning. Then, there was another job to be done.

Larmar had a hobby of ancient and modern weapons. A friend of his, Ellis Brown Mitchell, whom the gun world knew as Brownie, was at work cataloguing Larmar's extensive collection. Paul came in at eight o'clock and found Brownie in the gun room.

"Mr. Jordan said you'd help me." Brownie pushed an old percussion cap pistol to one side and looked up with a smile. He was a stocky compact fellow with sandy hair, scattered freckles, and soft gray eyes. In spite of his pudgy fingers, he handled every weapon he touched as if it were some priceless pearl.

"What do you want me to do?" Paul gazed distastefully at the assortment spread out on the broad flat-topped table and sat down.

Brownie took a sheaf of papers from a brief case on the floor.

"I've listed the rifles." He pointed to a gun rack on the wall where fifty or more flintlocks and carbines reposed in a military row. "There's a short history of each here. Mr. Jordan said you'd type them up—three carbons."

"There are always three carbons," said Paul. "The original goes out to his agent, he keeps one, and the other two help to fill up the files. Of course, I have to do something to earn a living you know."

"It takes some time for me to write things down," Brownie explained apologetically, and rather taken aback by Paul's unenthusiastic tone. "Mr. Jordan suggested that I'd make more speed if I ran over the pistols quickly and dictated their pedigree to you."

"The next job I get, I'll join a union," said Paul. He took the papers from Brownie and looked at them briefly. "Outside of this, and fifteen pages of handwritten manuscript to type tonight, I haven't anything else to do."

"I'm sorry," said Brownie, "but Mr. Jordan—"

"Oh, don't mind me." Paul got up, went into another room, and returned with notebook and pencils. "It's a pity when Larmar's old man died he didn't take these old guns along with him. I wouldn't give fifteen cents for the pistol that shot Aaron Burr."

"It was Alexander Hamilton," Brownie reminded him gently. "They fought a duel at Weehawken in eighteen hundred and four. They probably used Wogden's dueling pistols which were popular at that time."

"Hamilton would be just as dead if Burr had used a shotgun," Paul remarked without much interest. "Do we start on that thing?" He made himself comfortable at the table and pointed to the pistol by Brownie's left arm.

"Yes," said Brownie, "let's go. You can put this down—*One percussion cap pistol, Ketland and Company, eight inch barrel. Hammer broken, and ramrod missing. Otherwise a fine piece."*

Paul looked up from his notes with a frown. "When I get through with all this, what's Larmar going to use it for?"

"He said something about a work on ancient and modern firearms." Brownie leaned back and squinted across the table at Paul. "Also I suppose, like most collectors, he'd like to have a catalogue that's up to date."

"What sort of a book does he intend doing?"

"I'm not quite sure." Brownie was vague. "He suggested that we collaborate as soon as he found the time."

"Hmp!" grunted Paul. "Don't get your hopes up. It won't sell fifty copies if it's printed and besides that, Larmar will never find the time. You deal in these things, don't you?"

"Yes," said Brownie, "and Mr. Jordan has a very valuable collection here."

"You'd never know it," Paul shrugged. "What good is a catalogue unless you put the prices down?"

Brownie smiled. "The prices of such things are what they will bring, Mr. Hirst. Old guns are valued by many things, the name of the maker, the state of preservation, and rarity. Even those factors don't set any determinable value. When a wealthy collector wants some piece and wants it bad, he'll really go to town. Now here's something here." He picked up a flintlock pistol with a very large bore. "This is one of the best pieces Mr. Jordan owns. A Harpers Ferry flintlock caliber fifty-four."

"So what?" asked Paul.

Brownie handed him the pistol and he took it gingerly. "You'll notice, Mr. Hirst, that it's marked *Harpers Ferry, 1804.* That's very odd, as the first pistols produced in Harpers Ferry were made in eighteen hundred and six, and then there were only eight."

"What's it worth?"

Brownie slowly shook his head. "I've heard of one selling for five thousand dollars. This is an excellent specimen. It might even bring more."

Paul's black eyes were noncommittal as he put the pistol back on the table. A tenuous idea had taken shape in his mind and he found it worrying.

For a long time he had kept Larmar Jordan's personal accounts. His employer without explanation had taken the books from Paul and turned them over to a public accountant some six months before.

Paul lit a cigarette and said abruptly with pencil poised, "We're wasting time."

Brownie turned back to his guns and opened fire with a Le Mat nine shot revolver for metallic rifle cartridges with large bore under barrel for buckshot.

At Paul's grimace he said rather testily, "Le Mat supplied the Confederate officers during the Civil War."

"That's probably why they lost," said Paul.

It was close to 11:00 when he put his notebook down and escorted Brownie to the door. He strolled out onto the terrace after the gun expert had gone and stood for a time smoking with quick nervous puffs while he stared at the window of Lucia's room.

There had been no sign of the Jordans all evening. Paul decided they must have gone to a show together despite their tiff during the afternoon.

Harry came out and asked, "Is there anything more, Mr. Hirst?"

"Go to bed," said Paul.

"Good night, sir."

"Good night."

The houseman disappeared inside. Paul stretched himself out on the terrace divan, tossed his cigarette into the box of the privet hedge and watched it smolder and die. Winnie, the cocker, jumped up beside him demanding caresses with energetic pushes of a cold nose against his hand. Paul scratched him absently and the dog settled down.

Paul stared up at an incongruous moon that hung above surrounding buildings which looked soft and unreal against the starry sky. It was late and he was tired and he still had work to do, but somehow he couldn't keep the prospective typing on his mind.

If Lucia and Larmar split up, Paul would quit his job he knew. Lucia, at least, was occasionally gracious and it would be just too damn wearing to stay on placidly accepting continuous slights from Larmar. Or maybe he was oversensitive. His mind dropped back to Larmar's hiring an accountant six months before.

"A matter of income tax," his employer explained. But, Paul was pretty good on income tax himself. Still, it might be his own bitterness of feeling that made him read overt motives into anything done by Larmar.

There had been a lot of petty economies lately, particularly since Paul quit keeping the books. Cheaper brands of liquor. Carping about Lucia's bills. Sarcastic remarks over such trivial items as stationery. Paul had remarked on it once quite openly with the privilege of a confidential secretary, only to have Larmar say in his best flat tone of annoyance, "What the hell, Paul, haven't you heard that this country is involved in a war?"

Winnie jumped down and began a bark which instantly stopped. A door closed inside. Paul looked in through the study and saw that it was Larmar. He'd returned alone and quite drunk, unless the outward signs had been misinterpreted by Paul.

Larmar came toward the terrace staggering slightly as he threw his hat on one of the study settees.

"Harry," he called a trifle thickly.

"He's gone to bed, Mr. Jordan," said Paul. He stayed where he was on the terrace divan and spoke through the open door.

Larmar came out and collapsed in a blue and white chair. "That damn coon's always in bed when I want him. Get me a drink, will you, Paul?"

Paul got up, his lips set tight, and walked inside where a small bar set off the hall. He took ice from a vacuum, mixed a scotch and soda and had a quick one on his own. This might be the time. It was always an ordeal on the occasions when he had to contend with a drunken Larmar. Fortunately, the occasions were rare or Paul's career as a secretary wouldn't have gotten very far.

Paul came back out and said, "Harry's had double the work to do since you let the housemaid go, Mr. Jordan." He handed the drink to Larmar.

He wanted to ask about Lucia, but held his tongue, seating himself rigidly on the edge of the divan and waiting for something from Larmar.

The author gulped his drink. "I'll be lucky if everything doesn't disappear before the end of this war."

Paul said, staring at him through the semi-darkness, "Of course I haven't been keeping the books lately, but I thought you'd had a pretty good year."

"If you're wondering what happened to Lucia, she's dancing with that fat hog, Bob Morse." Larmar set his drink down on the flagstone terrace and lit a cigarette with a shaky hand.

"I'm sorry if I gave you any such impression," said Paul. "As a matter of fact, I've been wondering about Brownie Mitchell. I've been working with him all evening. Do you think this book you're contemplating with him is worth your time?"

"What book?" Larmar flicked ashes on the floor. "He's cataloguing my collection."

"Oh, then you're having to pay him. Isn't it rather expensive, Mr. Jordan, what with a bad year and the war?"

"I'm going to sell my guns, not that it's any of your business." Larmar got up and made wavery progress inside through the study door. "If you're up when Lucia comes in, tell her I'm asleep. Not that she'll care," he tossed back over his shoulder.

Paul lit another cigarette and smoked it slowly. It needed something catastrophic to make Larmar Jordan sell his prize collection. Something even greater in Larmar's life than a world-wide war.

4

Murder to Larmar Jordan, if he ever thought about it, was a privilege and pleasure of what he was pleased to call "tabloid society." It certainly had nothing to do with those preferred higher minds whose lives bounced gayly back and forth between penthouse and party. Some young fellow without either brains or initiative needed thirty cents for an indeterminate purpose, so he murdered the keeper of a crossroads store and dipped bloody fingers in the till. Or a moronic lad with a too high count of hormones spied a pretty schoolgirl tripping home in the afternoon and did a little stone bashing. Afterward he disposed of her body in the county reservoir.

These were matters for the heavy handed police and the fact-fiction magazines catering to readers who steeped themselves in the sordid side of crime. Allah be praised! Such things could never thrust their ugly heads up in the environs of the Arday Apartments.

Occasionally, it was true, Larmar heard of some wealthy man being murdered, or of some society matron passing out, clad only in crepe de chine pajamas and a veil of mystery. Such things made him shudder as though, coming out of the portals of a fashionable church on Sunday, he had collided forcibly into some drunken and verminous bum.

Guns were his hobby, things of beauty to him, made to treasure and admire, but not to shoot and kill. The son of a wealthy Philadelphia publisher, he had been reared in a Main Line house where a wing was set aside for his father's collection. He had mastered rifle and pistol shooting as a boy, competing on his high school and college teams and running up consistently high scores at the N. R. A., which stood for the National Rifle Academy and had nothing to do with the New Deal.

If his family had had less money, Larmar's childhood might have been more healthy. His father was a pedantic man of strong opinions, with little tolerance and less understanding of his son. Mrs. Jordan lived the slightly cowed life of an early century social butterfly. Larmar didn't particularly like his father, who bored him with stentorian phrases. And he hadn't much respect for his mother, who knew a lot about bridge and little about the multitudinous problems confronting a growing boy.

He turned to books and clung to them diligently, shutting out the world of reality until it was time for his parents to die. He became a joiner in school and college, a trait which he had carried over into later life. But it was only to prove his normalcy to the outside world. Once he was admitted to a fraternity or brotherhood his ego was satisfied and he made it a point seldom to attend a meeting. Actually, except for the companionship of the characters in his novels, Larmar Jordan was a very lonely man as he had been a very lonely boy.

He was twenty-eight when he married Lucia, a product of the flapper era and the youngest of a large family. Lucia had tired of receiving the cast-offs of older sisters and had learned how to use her large blue eyes effectively at the age of seventeen. Her judicious warming of the well-to-do Larmar under a blanket of flaming youth had successfully burned out his resistance to marriage in less than a year. Lucia, he knew, was proud of his work because it made money. She was proud of the apartment because it represented money. Highly resentful of any attentions which Larmar received from other women, she was equally proud of the attentions she received from other men. Larmar judged that she had been faithful, for Lucia was careful and hung on with turtle tenacity once she had a good thing.

After twelve years of marriage there were moments when he wanted nothing more in the world than to give her a good working over with a hairbrush. He had never been able to convince himself that in love, sex, work, or friendship, Lucia Jordan could be really sincere.

Larmar considered writing a business. If he never ascended to any great heights, he equally avoided the abysmal lows. After his first two books he had managed to lay out his working hours into a systematized routine—seldom interfered with by sorry memories of the night before. On the terrace in summer and in his study in winter, from two to six in the afternoon, he pro-

duced without too much effort some 2,000 words of fiction in
his cramped meticulous hand. That is to say, he had produced
before the disturbing advent of Troy Singleton upon his marital
scene.

Seated at his desk on the terrace on the afternoon following the
cocktail party, he was busily engaged in constructing a series of
boxes neatly connected with parallel lines while he thought about
Troy. Troy was a problem.

Larmar had met her a year before at a cocktail party in the
village. Oddly enough he had been introduced to her by Paul.
Lucia was away and Larmar, finding himself at loose ends on a
Saturday afternoon, had attached himself to his secretary. They
had finished up in two large basement rooms which opened onto
a garden. Larmar didn't even know the name of the people.
The only thing he remembered distinctly was that Troy stood
out from the crowd looking fresh, cool, and composed in an atmosphere as thick as steam.

The outside world was inclined to misjudge Larmar. He disliked serious involvements with women. Lucia might exasperate
and bore him but his love of the conventions was overpoweringly
strong. He enjoyed drinking discreetly with any new girl who
offered a mild flirtation. He might follow up with dinners,
theaters, and dancing, if he found himself particularly attracted—
but his interest was quick to wane.

Troy was different. In the first place, physically, she and Larmar Jordan contrasted to an extreme. Her classic face and
symmetrically round body had attracted him strongly. Then,
instead of gushing, she had passed him over with a word of
greeting and started an animated conversation with Paul.

There was a curious quality of ungrown-upness about Troy

which had proved that final barb necessary·to finally hook and hold the elusive Larmar. She could talk so frankly, so uninhibitedly, telling him everything about herself and her troubles, her black eyes softened with unuttered appeal.

There had been a lot of jobs, but no men, according to Troy. It might have been the truth. Larmar's most skillful tactics were handily defeated by her cloak of innocent girlishness. At any rate her technique had to be admired. In the short space of a year she had handily milked a fortune out of Larmar.

Making boxes on his pad out on the terrace he reached a most unhappy conclusion. Buried under Troy's artistically coifed black hair was the acme of a calculating brain.

Even with the income from his parents' estate, Larmar was not a wealthy man. Lucia was extravagant. In spite of consistently increasing income from his writing, household expenses and current bills kept his bank account pressing very close to the wall. Yet Larmar was canny and over a period of time he had managed to salt away in first-class securities quite a tidy sum.

That was before he met Troy.

First it had been a small matter of a few thousand dollars to get her a part in a show. The expenses of production had, unfortunately, exceeded the estimate. To save his initial investment, Larmar, egged on by Troy's almost suicidal disappointment, had been persuaded to put in more. The show died aborning but failed to kill his infatuation for Troy. With her deep dark eyes promising everything, she came to the rescue. Larmar could recoup his losses in the night club business. There were fortunes to be made since the war.

His work began to suffer under worry.

Troy was still as sweet and virginal as some early morning

blossom. By that time he realized that his gun collection was doomed and that there was more to opening a night club than merely unlocking the door.

Paul came out on the terrace and glanced accusingly at the pad of doodles. "What do you want?" Larmar asked. "You know I'm not supposed to be disturbed during the afternoon."

"You didn't seem busy," said Paul. "I've typed all the notes on the guns. I thought if you had anything to be copied I'd do it now. Sarah Hanley phoned. Said she had a bite on a serial. She wanted to know when you would have something to show her."

"When I get damned good and ready," said Larmar. "She thinks she can shake words out of me like a housemaid shakes dust from a broom."

"Well, it might be worth twenty-five thousand at that," Paul threw out by way of a feeler. "You could use it, couldn't you?"

Larmar discovered he had a headache. "Look, it's nearly four, Paul. You've been working hard all day, and I'm in a slump. Where's Lucia?"

"Out," said Paul.

"Well, you get out too, won't you? Let me alone. I want to think. You need a rest anyhow."

Paul stared at him for a second and touched his black mustache to hide a quirk at Larmar's unusual display of concern. "You'll want something as soon as I'm gone and Harry isn't here."

"Where the devil is he!"

Paul said, "This is Thursday, his afternoon."

"It's damn funny," said Larmar, "that *I* never get an afternoon. But of course, writers never work for a living anyhow. All they do is put things down."

"I think I better stay in," said Paul.

"Well, for the love of heaven, get out," Larmar told him with a frown. "Go uptown and walk around the reservoir or go get drunk in a bar."

"Okay," said Paul. "But don't start cussing me when you call."

Winnie trotted out on the terrace glancing hopefully from his master to Paul. "Shall I take the dog?"

"No," said Larmar. "Leave him. If he bothers me I'll shut him in Lucia's room."

He snapped his fingers. Winnie ran under the desk, found a place by his feet and settled down. Larmar wrote "Is this the face that launched a thousand ships," at the bottom of the page of doodles, then tore the whole thing off, crumpled it up into a ball, and threw it on the floor.

Sarah Hanley's phone call about a serial bite on his book had given him a mental prod. Words began to come. He lost himself in work for an hour and a half. It was after half past five when the doorbell rang. He stopped and listened while it trilled three times. Then, cursing softly, he remembered he was in the apartment alone, and went inside to answer the door.

The visitor was Troy, looking especially desirable in a light blue dress which defied the heat with a trimming of summer fur.

Larmar made no move to step aside. "I'm busy, darling. I thought we settled the matter of your coming here at the cocktail party yesterday afternoon."

She sensed his coldness and said, quite undisturbed, "I've come for the last time, Larmar. I thought it was a good chance to tell you something."

"If it's the last time it's just as well for everybody concerned," said Larmar. "I might as well tell you here and now, I'm broke."

"Easy come and easy go, Larmar." She shrugged, her eyes

unreadable. "Don't be so dramatic. We've had a bad run of luck, but you still may collect. That's what I wanted to talk to you about. That, and something else."

"I said I was broke." He still didn't move.

"You might as well let me in and listen. I won't stay long and I know you're here alone." She smiled an impish smile. "Your wife is having cocktails with a newspaper man. I saw her in Robertina's bar just a few minutes ago."

"Come in." Lamar's lips set in a cynical line. "Go on out on the terrace and sit down. I'll make us a couple of drinks." His face was drawn as he watched the swing of her figure going out the terrace door.

He had fixed a shaker of Martinis and put it on a silver tray with two crystal glasses, when the carillon across the street began to chime. As he stepped into the study carrying the tray, cutting through the brazen notes of the carillon came the sharp quick crack of a gun.

Out on the terrace Troy was seated in the metal chair in front of his desk. For an instant Larmar stopped—watching her through the open door. Then something about the way she slumped down slowly relaxed his fingers so that he dropped the cocktail tray.

He called to her once from the door. A single startled, "Troy!"

She sat quite motionless with never a word to say. Larmar crossed the terrace and stared at the neat round hole over her heart in the light blue dress where a spot of blood had widened and begun to trickle down.

Suddenly maddened, he tore through the privet hedge and leaned far over the wide stone coping. There was nothing there, of course, except a drop of six full stories, and another terrace below.

He turned to the desk, touched her, again said softly, "Troy."
Across the street the carillon began another hymn.
Somewhere out of the past, Larmar found himself remembering the words of an old-time song:

"Tolling for the outcast,
  Tolling for the gay,
  Tolling for the millionaire
  And friends long passed away,
  And my heart is light and gay
  As I stroll down old Broadway
  When I'm listening to the chimes of Trinity."

" . . . 'tis not to come;"

I

MANY EXCELLENT books have been written setting forth in some detail the procedure of a trained investigator when he arrives at the scene of murder. Messrs. Soderman and O'Connell, in their comprehensive volume on modern criminal investigation, state succinctly as Number One: "Ascertain who the perpetrator is and arrest immediately if possible."

Fortunately or unfortunately, depending upon the point of view, no textbook has ever been issued to cover adequately the correct procedure of a murderer. Possibly the scope is too broad. It would be most difficult to enclose in the pages of a single volume the best routine to follow when one gazes down for the first time at the blanched countenance of a freshly poisoned wife, a newly stabbed sweetheart, or the still exquisite though lifeless form of a recently shot inamorata seated quite stolidly in one's terrace chair.

It was a stupefying moment at best for Larmar Jordan, one scarcely productive of the clear and logical thinking which had made his books a success. Troy Singleton was dead. The seconds were ticking along. He had seen her walk out very much alive a very few minutes before. The terrace dropped down in steep unscalable walls fourteen stories on each side and six at the back to another terrace below.

Held with a terrific clamp of fascination, Larmar took a step closer and looked at her again, watching the widening stain on her dress and the play of setting sunlight on her hair.

The chimes in the church were still ringing. He turned and stared up vacuously, letting his eyes climb tier by tier to where the Arday Apartments ended in a tower on the twentieth floor. Several windows were opened in the apartments above. Enough gumption and gun lore returned for him to realize that Troy's wound would have been in the back had she been shot from a window above. Numb, and fighting a losing battle to contain himself, he went behind his desk and sat down.

He had to leave immediately, unable to face Troy's eyes, half closed in a dead accusing stare.

A tidal wave of disbelief swept over him scourging him into action. The girl was dead, shot through the heart. Bullets didn't come out of thin air.

Moved by a spasm approaching insanity, he dashed into the apartment and tore from room to room, peering under beds, flinging open doors and thrusting clothing aside in the closets.

The carillon stopped.

Winnie came in and followed him about barking excitedly at this new-found game. His jumping nerves in a livid painful tangle, Larmar cursed the dog and shut him up in Lucia's room. Stiff legged, walking like an old man, he returned to the terrace.

Summoning a doctor seemed the logical thing to do. Larmar went inside, sat down, and reached for the phone by the study divan. He discarded it, picking up the telephone directory instead and leafing feverishly through its pages until the Smiths came to view. There were literally hundreds of Smiths. Battalions of them as similar as soldiers, ranked up and down the pages in orderly columns. For the life of him he couldn't remember whether his personal physician was J. George or George J. As for the telephone number, which he normally knew quite well, it had taken flight along with the doctor's address. A laborious search through the G's and J's finally unearthed the elusive doctor.

Larmar dialed the number and sat staring at the back of Troy's head. It wouldn't have surprised him had she stood up, flashed her impish smile at him, and walked away.

"Dr. George J. Smith's office," said a voice on the phone.

"I want to speak to the doctor."

"I'm sorry. The doctor's hours are from nine to one. May I have your name?"

"No," said Larmar, filled with a new-found caution. The voice on the telephone irritated him with its happy unconcern. "Do you think I might find him at home? This is a personal call."

"I'm sorry," said the voice, "but Dr. Smith is away. If it's an emergency, Dr. Harvey is handling his practice. I can give you Dr. Harvey's phone number or I can take a message."

"Skip it," said Larmar. "His wealthiest patient is dying of a burst appendix, that's all." He hung up with a scowl.

Damn doctors anyway. They were like policemen. Let something serious happen and none was to be found.

His hand felt cold and clammy as he released the telephone. The thought of policemen had started his active imagination jumping up and down. His only contact with the police force had been through the rather impersonal medium of tickets attached to his car.

Wild stories of departmental procedure flooded back to haunt him. Murderers were loaded down with chains and removed to the soundless vastness of subterranean vaults. There they were seated under the burning glare of electric lights, while half a dozen members of the strong arm squad worked them over with rubber blackjacks and lengths of hose. If a confession was not promptly forthcoming, the murderer's battered carcass might disappear into the headquarter's files—never to be found.

The apartment was frighteningly silent.

"God above! I didn't kill her," he said aloud. His own voice upset him still more by its raucous unnatural sound.

He started to analyze the situation with what at the moment seemed to be sound common sense.

A girl was shot on your terrace, but you didn't do it.

She was instantly killed.

Or was she?

Larmar got up with a groan, dashed into Lucia's room and started searching for a hand mirror. Winnie jumped up on him and greeted him. He cowered when Larmar sternly ordered him down. He found a gold-backed mirror on the dressing table, shut the dog up again and returned to Troy.

The mirror, held close to her full red lips without a wisp of her breath to mar its surface, stayed as clear as a summer dawn. Obviously something had to be done. Paul would return any minute, and Lucia, too. His failure to call the police might be damning. He went back into the study and again sat down.

Once more his imagination checked him, holding back his wrist with the cold bony fingers of logic, as he reached for the telephone. He evolved an imaginary page of dialogue:

"Police headquarters? This is Larmar Jordan, the Arday Apartments, Tenth Street and Fifth Avenue. A girl's just been shot on my terrace."

"Accident?"

"I don't know."

"Oh, you don't know. We'll send someone right over. Hold any witnesses that are around."

"Well, er—there aren't any witnesses."

"Then don't let anybody leave until we get there."

"But I'm the only one here."

"You mean you were the only one there when she was shot?"

"Yes, that's right. But you see, I didn't kill her."

"Oh, you didn't kill her. Then who did?"

"Well, somebody shot her. He must have been on the other side of the terrace wall at the back."

"And what's on the other side of the wall?"

"Oh well, nothing except a straight drop of six stories."

"We'll be right over. And say, Mr. Jordan . . ."

"Yes."

"You'd better wait there. If it's six stories to the next terrace, we might like to have you explain just how the murderer climbed down."

It didn't sound too hot. He looked at himself in the hand mirror and found that his eyes were strained and his face a pasty gray. Disgustedly he put the mirror down on the stand by the telephone.

"To hell with the police," he muttered.

He'd never been involved in a murder before, but he was up to his ears in one now. Larmar Jordan had a definite hunch that by some hook or crook he'd better get Troy Singleton's body out of the way.

Troy's apartment was on East Eighty-first Street uptown. It was served by an automatic elevator and the small lobby was almost always deserted. Whipped into panic by his own unhappy cogitations, Larmar determined to get her there even if he had to call on Paul. It was a job for after dark.

In the meantime, he couldn't very well leave her slumped in that grotesque position in the metal chair. He dismissed the idea of hiding her in Lucia's room. There was the matter of blood stains to contend with, and he hadn't much faith in Lucia's nerves. Lucia always believed the worst of him. She'd mark him guilty with never a chance to explain.

He went into the gun room and covered the broad, flat table with newspapers taken from a pile which Harry kept in the kitchen.

Brownie was due at eight that night to catalogue more guns, but Brownie could be put off by a telephone call.

Back on the terrace, it took a moment to nerve himself before he could lift Troy from the chair. Then he found her incredibly heavy. Staggering under her weight, he made his way back through the study into the hall. Once in the gun room he stretched her out on the paper-covered table, then closed and locked the door, pocketing the key.

With a dampened paper towel, he went back over his tracks, picking up an occasional blood drop. Later he was to learn that despite his care, he hadn't found them all. He wet another towel and cleaned the white metal garden chair. Satisfied for the moment, he washed his hands in the bathroom and flushed the towels down the drain. The broken glasses he retrieved from the study floor, mopping up the spilled Martinis as best he could. The pieces of broken glass went into the covered kitchen garbage pail.

Larmar was moving in a terrible kind of dream, but out of it he had conceived a plan for Troy. Due to the shortage of help, there was no man on duty at night in the service elevator at the end of the hall. He would take her down there, out through the basement into the alley, and load her into his car.

Somehow, of course, he must rid himself for the evening of Lucia's presence and possibly of Paul's.

The doorbell rang.

Larmar lit a cigarette and dragged on it deeply before he placed it on an ash tray and went to answer.

Two men were standing outside, a massive one with a round kindly face and friendly blue eyes, and a thinner one, with sharp gray eyes and hair touched white at the temples. The massive man wore blue serge, double-breasted and well cut; the thinner man was clad in an expensive light suit of gray.

"Yes?" said Larmar, uncomfortably conscious that the color in his face and lips was draining slowly away.

"Are you Mr. Jordan?" asked the man in gray.

"Yes."

"I'm Inspector Larry Davis of the New York Homicide Squad and this is Sergeant Archer. Has there been some trouble here?"

"None that I know of," said Larmar frostily.

"Well, then you don't mind if we come in, I'm sure." The inspector's clipped mustache moved upward with a semblance of a smile. "I dislike to disturb you, but a Mrs. Oliver in the apartment above you became alarmed."

"At what?" asked Larmar, and wet his lips.

"I'm sure I don't know," said Davis, pushing the door gently inward. "Whatever it was, she thought enough of it to turn in a homicide call."

2

The inspector came inside and walked through the hall into the study with the friendly unconcern of a bosom friend making a most informal call. The sergeant followed, closing the hall door behind him, and pasting his heavy shoulders against it. Standing there, he had the immutable consistency of some impassive wall.

Larmar discovered that his brain was working with lightning-like speed, galloping along jerkily to unroll a panorama as though some ancient newsreel film was being exhibited in the darkness of his head, depicting unpleasant events both past and to come.

Standing in the foyer with Archer blocking the door, and the suave untroubled Davis looking admiringly about the study, he had a sensation of being pressed unhappily in a sandwich composed of two impersonal representatives of the New York law.

Davis crossed the study and sat down.

A series of sharp staccato barks from Lucia's room announced that Winnie had recognized an unfamiliar footfall.

"Sounds like a dog," said Archer.

Larmar brushed him off with a single withering glance and stepped into the study from the hall.

The inspector discovered a mirrored cigarette box on the top of the coffee table. Using it like a vanity case, he proceeded to examine his clipped mustache with care.

"Nice place you have here, Mr. Jordan." He put the box down and looked out over the terrace.

"Thanks," said Larmar shortly. "I am sure Mrs. Jordan would like you and the sergeant to drop in some time and pay us a social call."

The inspector's gray mustache moved ever so slightly, telegraphing a grin.

"You'd be surprised how many screwy calls come into the New York Police Department in a single day."

"I doubt it," said Larmar, and took a cigarette from the mirrored box pushing it closer to Davis with a gesture of invitation.

The inspector declined with a wave of one capable hand.

"Come on in, Archer," he called to the sergeant. "Nice place Mr. Jordan has here. Maybe he can find you a cigar."

The sergeant came in and sat down.

"There is a humidor in that table beside you," said Larmar.

Archer opened it and took out a cigar. He lit it with a nod of thanks and breathed out a great cloud of blue-white smoke.

Larmar recognized that his irritation was mounting, sand-papering his self-control until every nerve was raw. There was some definite line to take but he couldn't find it. He was too acutely conscious of Troy Singleton's body spread out on newspapers in the gun room. Repartee seemed scarcely adequate as a means of postponing the inevitable investigation. Both his unwelcome visitors appeared to have a sense of humor but it bordered on the macabre. Larmar doubted that it would carry over to palliate the threatened discovery of Troy.

Winnie had another spasm of barking.

The two officers had lapsed into a comfortable silence. Archer smoked placidly. The inspector found a toothpick and reduced it to a miniature strand of whisk broom, an operation which he performed with ruminating relish.

"Your dog wants out," said Archer.

"Damn the dog!" exploded Larmar. "I wish you two would state your business and get out. My wife's due home and I don't want her to find you here."

"I don't blame you," said Davis. He got up, put the toothpick in an ash tray, and casually walked across and felt the wet spot on the rug.

"Spill something?" he asked, as he straightened up.

"Cocktail," said Larmar and nearly bit off his tongue.

The inspector sniffed at his fingers. "It's the devil to get gin nowadays. I hate to see it wasted."

He walked to the foyer and looked at the closed door of the gun room but made no move to try it. Instead he stared over to the right and remarked, "That's a neat little bar."

"I'm glad you like my home," said Larmar. "I have no desire in the world to buck the intricate methods of the New York Police Department and I must admit I have a very inadequate knowledge of the law. Still, I would like to ask a question. Have you a search warrant?"

The inspector wiped his fingers on a large square of spotless linen before he replied. Then it was only to ask Larmar sadly, "What would we want a search warrant for?"

"I believe you need one to go barging into people's homes."

"Barging?" The inspector's eyebrows shot together in a V of inquiry. "Have we been barging, Archer?"

"Not that I know of," said the sergeant. "Mr. Jordan even gave me a cigar."

"I'll tell you how it is," said Davis breaking out with a rash of fatherly concern. "We have certain duties to perform and we like to do them without causing any trouble. Now this lady upstairs, Mrs. Oliver—do you know her?"

"I've seen her once or twice in the downstairs hall."

"Well, she's probably a nosy old wench," Davis continued. "I doubt whether she ever drinks or smokes."

"Suppressed like," said Archer, and de-ashed his cigar.

The inspector's gray eyes crinkled. "You understand, Mr. Jordan. She's the type of a dame who shudders every time she passes a bar. Her windows overlook your terrace. You have cocktail parties there occasionally and the sight of so much joy burns up this Mrs. Oliver. So what does she think when she sees a beautiful black-haired girl collapse in a terrace chair?"

"You're fascinating me," said Larmar. "What does she think?"

The inspector laughed softly. "She thinks that she heard a shot, Mr. Jordan. She knows this young lady isn't your wife and she can't possibly understand that young ladies who collapse in chairs instead of being shot, have usually gotten half-shot at a bar."

Larmar realized that his pent-up breath had been causing his heart to pound, giving him a certain amount of pain. He drew in smoke and released it very slowly, speaking through the casual trickle.

"I don't see that I'm called upon to involve myself or anyone else, Inspector."

"Of course not," Davis agreed. "You carried the young lady inside. She's probably sleeping it off in another room. We'll just take a look. Not even disturb her, see. As a matter of fact, we haven't seen anything." His shoulders raised in a tiny shrug. "Then Archer and I go home and have dinner and we don't have to bother you again at all."

"This is—"

"Preposterous," Davis supplied. "I agree one hundred per cent, Mr. Jordan. That's the penalty of living in a big city. A man can't even have a few drinks without some busybody sticking her nose in. It's that sort of thing that gives the Police Department a pain."

"And suppose I tell you that this young lady's gone home? Assuming a young lady was here."

A clock struck half past six.

"We'd call it a miracle," said Sergeant Archer. He pushed his bulk up out of the chair and relinquished his cigar. "I've spent a long time on the force and I've learned a lot about lady lushes. They have rubber legs. I've never seen one yet who wasn't good for eight hours of sweet sound sleep once she slides down in a chair."

He turned his broad back on Larmar and Davis and moved on surprisingly light feet to the terrace door.

Larmar suppressed a demanding inclination to yell at the impassive sergeant, "Come back here! You mustn't go out there!"

A key clicked in the front door, sending Winnie into a renewed spasm of muffled barks and a frenzied scratching on the door of Lucia's room. Laughter and quick conversation followed.

"Christ almighty," muttered Larmar. A pang of emptiness akin to nausea had clutched at his stomach. Lucia gently pushing Bob Morse ahead of her came into the hall.

Lucia's blue eyes were sparkling with the overtones of two or three Martinis but Morse was surprisingly sober.

He grinned at Davis and said, "You certainly meet the most interesting people when you write for a living. What are all the ferrets out for, Inspector? Did somebody die?"

Davis shook hands. "I haven't seen you for a couple of years, Bob. Are you still on the *Globe-Tribune?*"

"Part time," said Morse. His searching glance had left the inspector and was following Sergeant Archer who had stepped out onto the terrace.

Lucia studied her husband for a moment, then unexpectedly stepped closer to him and pecked at his cheek, leaving a smudge of lipstick.

"You look tired, darling. Bob says you promised to do more work with him tonight on the profile."

"I am tired." Larmar was also watching the sergeant who had pushed his girth through the privet hedge and was staring down over the terrace wall.

The shadows outside were sharpening, softening the colored stripes of the awning above Larmar's desk. They deepened the orange umbrellas above the tables until they looked almost crimson.

"There was some trouble upstairs," said Larmar. "This is

Inspector Davis from Police Headquarters. He dropped in to see if I'd heard anything."

The inspector nodded tacitly and draped himself against the back of a sofa.

"Police Headquarters?" Lucia looked pale as she put a hand on Larmar's arm and turned to face Davis. "This apartment house is unusually well built. There have been plenty of parties in the other apartments, but we never hear a sound."

"I'm sure you don't," said Davis.

Lucia suddenly changed her air.

"Why don't you mix us some cocktails, darling? Then you and Bob and I can go out to dinner. Skip the profile for tonight. You don't seem to feel very well."

Out on the terrace the sergeant rounded Larmar's desk and pushed through the privet hedge to once more stare down over the wall. He stood there for a moment, bulking large against the sky.

Lucia opened her bedroom door and let out Winnie who dashed about excitedly seeking attention from his mistress and Larmar. When Larmar looked out on the terrace again, the sergeant had apparently gone.

"He's crawling around in back of your desk," said Morse, as though Larmar had asked him a question. "I wonder what he's looking for."

"He's an inquisitive cuss, Archer." The inspector left his post by the sofa and without a glance at anyone, walked quickly out to join the sergeant.

Lucia asked, "What's all this about, Larmar?"

Before he could answer, Davis called from the terrace, "Would you come here just a moment, Mr. Jordan?"

The tone of the request was entirely too smooth. It touched

a nerve at the base of Larmar's spine and seemed to paralyze him completely. He stood, not moving, until he realized Morse was looking at him with something more than casual interest and Lucia said,

"He wants you to come out there, Larmar."

"Certainly," he said; and walked out to join Davis and Archer.

Like the day before when he had escorted Troy across the terrace, the distance seemed terribly far. He stopped by his desk, suppressing a desire to look back over his shoulder and see if Lucia and Morse were watching.

Archer was on his knees, and his heavy hands had parted the springy bushes of the privet hedge. Larmar followed the line of the inspector's finger which was casually pointing down.

A handkerchief had caught on a twig and hung there limply. Close beside it, lying starkly against the dampened soil in the narrow green box which held the hedge was a strange looking long barreled pistol.

"Did you ever see that before?" the inspector asked him flatly.

"It's a Buchel target pistol," said Larmar unbelievingly.

"I didn't ask you what it was," said Davis, "I asked you if you had ever seen it before."

"Certainly," said Larmar. "I've shot it hundreds of times and won three cups with it."

"It's yours?"

"Of course," said Larmar, "it's mine."

It was funny. It had never occurred to him that whoever shot Troy Singleton would certainly have used a gun.

"Of course," he repeated with lips gone stiff and dry, "of course it's mine."

Davis leaned against the desk edge and groped for another toothpick. Once he had it he broke it into two equal pieces, then broke the two into four. Without any warning he reached out quickly and closed his fingers about Larmar's right arm turning the bottom of the coatsleeve into view.

"That's blood on your cuff, Mr. Jordan," he said. "Let's quit horsing. What did you do with the body of that girl?"

3

"So they're holding him for murder?" said Duncan Maclain.

Paul Hirst, more or less swallowed in the depths of a red leather armchair, let his black eyes rove about the paneled walls of the Captain's penthouse office before he replied. Finding no inspiration in the impersonal oak paneling, he looked toward Lucia, seated beside Sybella Ford on a wide divan. She turned her head away, refusing to meet his gaze.

"That's it," said Paul shortly. "Murder." He swung back slowly and resumed his study of Captain Maclain.

It was hot outside but the air-conditioned office was cool, as though the very room reflected a trace of the Captain's imperturbable unruffled calm.

The morning sunlight streamed in, cut into diamonds by the panes of glass set in the doors to the penthouse terrace. One of the diamonds fell directly across the perfect, sightless eyes of Duncan Maclain.

Paul had a sense of exasperation, directed against the blind man. It crept out and included Sybella Ford who had persuaded Lucia to ask the Captain's aid. He had agreed to talk with them readily enough, but Paul liked action.

Lucia's hysterical story, poured out in a torrent, had brought only a single question—"So they're holding him for murder?"— from the impassive Duncan Maclain.

"Larmar insists he didn't kill that girl and I believe him," said Lucia after a time.

A muscle moved lightly in the Captain's mobile face. He interlocked his long sensitive fingers and placed his folded hands on the edge of the desk with the posture of a child in school.

Again the office was silent to a point of strain.

"For God's sake, isn't there anything you can do to help him?" Paul demanded when the waiting had become unendurable.

"You're a very impetuous young man," said Duncan Maclain. He took a cigarette from a cloisonné box on the desk and flashed his lighter, touching the flame to the tip with the skillful ease of long practice.

"Mr. Jordan has been good to me," said Paul. "You'd be impetuous yourself if you were stuck in a filthy jail for something you didn't do, Captain Maclain."

The Captain traced a pattern on the desk top with his finger tip.

"Every conversation in this office is recorded on wax by a dictaphone set in the wall," he remarked quite generally. "I often find it necessary to hear what's said in here again and again."

"There hasn't been much said so far," said Paul.

"I disagree with you, Mr. Hirst," said Duncan Maclain. "The New York Homicide Squad is a startlingly efficient machine. I feel forced to tell you something even at the risk of causing Sybella and Mrs. Jordan a certain amount of pain. I've known Inspector Davis and worked with him for years. He's usually right."

"This time he isn't, Duncan," Sybella remarked softly.

The Captain gave a rueful smile.

"A woman's intuition pitted against the New York Homicide

Squad is a feeble thing. I'm unable to see, but I've heard Lucia's story and Rena Savage, my secretary, has read all the morning papers to me. The truth of the matter is that I'm not a wizard, and the facts sound very black, Sybella." He folded his hands again and added, "As a matter of fact, they're just about as black as can be."

"And still I don't believe Larmar killed her," said Lucia speaking wearily.

"Why?" asked Maclain.

Lucia moistened her lips.

"You say you've known Davis for many years. Well, I've lived with Larmar Jordan for many years. He values one thing above all others in life—his standing. Add to that the fact that he's smart, almost brilliant. He's worked like a slave to make a name in writing. If he was going to kill, he'd at least kill cleverly. I've accused him of many things, Captain Maclain, but I've never accused him of rank stupidity."

"I'm afraid he's already proved himself guilty of it," said Duncan Maclain. "Let's for a moment assume as the truth an item of the very highest improbability. Let's assume that Troy Singleton was shot on the terrace of your apartment by some unknown person whom your husband failed to see. Knowing himself not guilty, Mrs. Jordan, why did he carry the body inside and lock it in the gun room? Can you answer that question for me?"

"He was scared," said Paul.

"Then it seems to me he would have called for help," the Captain protested gently. "If he's as brilliant as you say, he certainly must know that the police can read such a story with the greatest of facility."

"They've been known to read things wrong," Sybella told him. "Witness the last case you worked on."

"That was one of the times," said Maclain, "that the police and I happened to disagree."

"Meaning that now you agree," said Paul.

"I haven't talked to the police, Mr. Hirst, but let's take a look at the cold hard facts since you and Mrs. Jordan have paid me the compliment of consulting me."

The telephone rang.

Lucia got up hurriedly and said, "That may be for me."

The Captain spoke briefly into the mouthpiece and then handed her the phone.

"It's Jess Ferguson, Larmar's attorney," Lucia said after a few words. "He's downstairs, Captain Maclain. Do you mind if he comes up? I asked him to call here for me."

"Not at all," the Captain assured her. "As a matter of fact there's nothing I'd like better than to be able to help you and Larmar. Perhaps Mr. Ferguson can do what you and Mr. Hirst have failed to do—persuade me that any attempt to clear your husband of this charge isn't an utter impossibility."

With a terse, "Come up, Jess," Lucia hung up the phone and sat down.

Schnucke, who had been basking in the sun in front of the diamond-paned doors, stood up and stretched with a pinkish yawn, then came to Maclain and put her head on his knee.

He gently scratched the top of her nose and said, "Lie down."

The buzzer rang in the anteroom. A moment later, Rena Savage ushered in a tall man in a seersucker suit. He acknowledged Lucia's introduction to Maclain by brightening his narrow sardonic face with the tiniest wisp of a smile.

As a practitioner of criminal law, Jess Ferguson had few equals, but Paul Hirst disliked his sloppiness on the few occasions when Ferguson had paid the Jordan's a call. Today was no exception.

The seersucker suit gave unspoken evidence of too many hours of wear.

The lawyer sat down and immediately increased his resemblance to a frizzled chicken by further mussing his shock of sandy unkempt hair.

"I hope you can unearth something to help us, Captain."

Ferguson's voice betrayed the secret of his great success. It played on a listener's emotions with the power of an organ in a dim cathedral. Under its mellifluous hammerings, adverse witnesses had been known actually to faint in the witness chair.

The Captain, who judged his fellow men by sounds, was quick to tabulate Jess Ferguson as part charlatan and part genius. Whatever the charlatan part might be, there was a wealth of honest sincerity there.

"I've been telling Lucia and Paul Hirst that I'm afraid I can't help them," said Duncan Maclain.

"Come now, Captain, nothing's quite that hopeless." The lawyer reached for his ear and plucked energetically at a tuft of pinkish hair.

"I'm afraid this is," Maclain announced without a change of tone. "You've been engaged to defend Larmar Jordan on a charge of murder. I think you'll do better to leave me out. I've reached the conclusion that at the time Troy Singleton was shot your client was the only one there."

"Now wait a minute," said Ferguson, and squirmed around in his chair. "I've just come from talking to Larmar. He's told me the truth—to that I'm ready to swear. Let's take the bad facts." He began to tick them off on his fingers. "The woman upstairs, Mrs. Evelyn Oliver, thought she heard a shot about the time the carillon started to ring. She went to the window and saw Troy

Singleton slumped down in a terrace chair. Now, mark this, Captain Maclain, if this woman saw nobody leave the terrace, are you ready to admit that Larmar wasn't there? For your information, whoever shot Troy Singleton was in front of her. The police are basing their case on that. They feel they can prove that the bullet was fired across the desk by someone sitting in Larmar's desk chair."

"It hasn't been proved that he didn't go inside before Mrs. Oliver got to the window," said Duncan Maclain.

"No," admitted Ferguson, "it hasn't." He further rumpled his hair. "But let's take other means of escape from the terrace. Through your room, Mrs. Jordan." He swung around on Lucia.

"Why, yes," she said in a frightened voice, "if Larmar had been in the study as he says, a man could have gone into my room from the terrace and hidden in there."

The Captain locked his hands behind his head and leaned back in his chair.

"You're about to add, I'm sure, that when your husband went out on the terrace this murderer left your bedroom by the inside door, slipped through the study and out into the apartment house hall."

Jess Ferguson sat up straight and said triumphantly, "You've proved my point, Captain Maclain, clinched it right there."

"Except for one thing." The Captain rocked himself slowly back and forth. "This morning I talked to Bob Morse of the *Globe-Tribune*. Knowing Larmar and Lucia, I was interested enough to call him on the telephone. According to Larmar's own story, which he told the police last night, he heard the shot, walked out onto the terrace and almost immediately sat down in his chair where he could easily have seen anyone who passed through the study. Immediately he got up again and rushed into Lucia's room where he looked under beds and through the closets." The Captain paused.

"What are you trying to prove?" asked Paul.

"I'm showing you that there was no one in Mrs. Jordan's room immediately after Troy was shot," said Duncan Maclain. "I'm showing you further that nobody went through her room from the terrace after Larmar Jordan searched it."

"How do you know?" asked Ferguson.

"I know," said Maclain, "because I own dogs. When Mrs. Jordan came back to the apartment last evening, she opened the door to her bedroom and Winnie ran out to greet her. Winnie, like most cockers, hates to be shut up anywhere. I'm afraid, Mr. Ferguson, that if an escaping murderer had opened that bedroom door—" The Captain paused and spread his hands expressively.

"You're right," said Ferguson grimly. "That dog would have been out of there quick as a bat out of hell!" He stood up. "I thought you might help. I'm sorry, but since you believe Larmar guilty I won't waste your time and mine."

"I haven't even intimated that I believe him guilty," said Duncan Maclain. "I've merely said the facts were black. As a matter of fact there are a couple of things about this shooting that cause me to think he's innocent."

"Such as?" Ferguson hitched up his rumpled trousers and sat down.

"The two broken cocktail glasses that Lucia mentioned," said Captain Maclain.

4

The Captain lived in a world of sound and blackness, a world where the continuity of existence was affected only slightly by the risings and the settings of the sun.

He had driven himself unremittingly for more than twenty years to overcome the handicap of blindness; two decades of effort where the lowest depths of weariness were doubled in intensity by the darkness; two long sevenths of a man's allotted span full of mileposts marked by finger tips tender from training themselves in the sense of touch, muscles wracked with disciplined exercise, keen ears deafened by ten thousand shots from an automatic while he learned to shoot at sound.

That was the road that Duncan Maclain had chosen to follow. It was a road made rough by the heavy sharp stones of disappointment. Every bypath led to danger and he had met but few companions on the way.

Spud and Rena were the closest, ever ready to aid him across the boggy expanse of discouragement's treacherous slough. Next came his Negro servants, Sarah Marsh, who cooked his meals and kept his house, and her giant chauffeur-valet husband, Cappo.

Schnucke and Driest, his German shepherds, could scarcely be called companions for they were a part of Duncan Maclain. Schnucke, smart and gentle, was his eyes. Driest, smart and fierce as a caged up tiger, was his bodyguard and weapon, as dangerous as a loaded gun.

The road had been long and difficult and lonely. He'd traveled far, far down it before love for a woman had come.

He loved Sybella Ford for many things. He couldn't see her beauty but her brain was quick and clear, accepting his blindness with never a hint of pampering. He liked her around him. Her presence in a room was fresh and clean like a distant breath of an orchard in early spring. He adored the sound of her voice, which was husky and caressing, a voice that would always be young. There was contentment in the touch of her soft cool fingers against his cheek.

Duncan Maclain was in love and afraid.

He had a goal at the end of the road—to prove himself as good as, or better than, any man with eyes. He of all people living knew in his heart that the goal was the foot of a rainbow which might never be attained. He was filled with frightful doubts that any woman, even Sybella Ford, could have the strength to survive the journey with him.

He had traveled the rough dark trail alone for twenty years. Now, past forty, he was more than acquainted with its perils. The end would never be in sight, for even after twenty years the journey had just begun.

There was no power of divination, no necromancy, no sixth sense to help the reasoning powers of Captain Duncan Maclain. His hunches grew out of cold, hard facts, scrutinized individually through a high-powered mental microscope whose lenses were composed of devastating concentration. Once blown up to reveal their component parts, the facts were rolled and patted and squeezed on every side until at last they became smooth and round and perfect and bright as a ball of crystal. The only gazing the Captain did to get his hunches was into that crystal ball.

He had a hunch about the murder of Troy. It was an unformed thing, quite nebulous, nothing much more than a few rough spots which marred the surface of the crystal ball. Yet, it started an anticipatory tingling at the base of the Captain's spine.

Problems were more heady and pleasurable to him than a draught of fine old whisky. The array of secondhand facts in his possession promised something more than a problem should he attempt to clear Larmar Jordan.

Every pointer indicated that the end might be a dank and dismal failure. Still, more because the Jordans were Sybella's friends than through any great feeling of confidence in the outcome, the Captain decided to take it on. He dismissed his four visitors with a rather vague promise to do what he could.

Once they were gone, he dialed Spring 7-3100 with lightning rapidity and after a moment's wait got Davis on the phone.

"Haven't you been killed yet?" the inspector asked him cheerfully.

"Nobody dares, Larry." The Captain hid a grin. "Every murderer who thirsts for my blood is afraid to take a chance. They know that the odds of your catching them are ten to one."

"Look," said Davis, "save your arithmetical insults for Archer. I'm trying to run a Homicide Bureau and time's catching up with me." He paused and chuckled. "The prospective frying of a certain Larmar Jordan in the hot seat wouldn't be the reason for this telephone call, would it, Maclain?"

"Jordan?" the Captain repeated innocently. "Never heard of him. I just thought I hadn't seen you and that captive balloon you travel around with for a month of Sundays. It occurred to me if you weren't doing anything you might drop in sometime today and have a drink."

"Now that's right white of you, podner," the inspector assured him with a fine West-Brooklyn accent. "You're also the biggest liar between the Battery and the Bronx. You attended a cocktail party at the Jordans' day before yesterday."

"Gad," said the Captain, "it's getting so with that Centre Street Gestapo that a man can't make a social call."

The inspector grew confidential.

"Look, Maclain, we've been friends for a long time. There're certain things about my job I hate. One of them is hauling in a pretty decent sort of a guy for burning down a nasty little frail like that Singleton dame."

"Why Larry Davis, you've been reading the pulps," said Duncan Maclain. "I only heard about Larmar Jordan this morning, and you already have him tried and convicted."

"I'm merely trying to save you from wearing out your dog's tender feet," the inspector continued quite amiably. His voice grew more serious. "I'm telling you if you mix yourself up in this you'll go against your own good judgment when you hear the facts. You're too damn smart to become involved in a mess like this out of friendship. You've helped us a lot, Captain, and I'd hate to see you fail. But this is open and shut. It hasn't any angles. It hasn't any mystery. It's just plain tabloid about a guy who bumped off his frail."

"Then I'm sure that you and Archer won't mind coming up and giving me the low-down," said Duncan Maclain. "It might keep me out and it certainly can't get Larmar out of jail."

He hung up gently and sat for a long time drumming his fingers on the polished black rubber of the telephone. Finally he got up and selected three records from the mahogany cabinet where the discs were indexed in Braille. He put them on the Capehart, set the changer, started the machine and stretched out full length on the wide divan.

A few minutes later Rena stuck her head in, saw that he was lost in *Scheherazade,* and softly closed the door. The records played through and stopped. Still Maclain lay motionless, relaxed in every muscle.

Half an hour later he sat up straight and rigid when the buzzer anteroom rang.

Rena opened the door and said, "Those men are here again."

The Captain raised his eyebrows and listened to the double set of footsteps, soft on the thick pile carpet. He stood up, grinned, and walking to a panel in the corner, pushed it back, disclosing a compact hidden bar.

Leather creaked protestingly as Sergeant Archer relaxed his bulk in a chair.

"It's nice of you fellows to come up and save me from making a fool of myself," the Captain remarked. "I'll let you fix the drinks, Davis." He hooked a thumb toward the bar, then went to his desk and sat down.

The inspector clinked ice in glasses and poured Scotch for them all, chuckling in rare good humor as he put a drink on the Captain's desk and passed another to Archer.

"You sound hilarious for an Irish sourpuss, Larry." The Captain sipped his highball and lit a cigarette.

"I'm feeling pretty good about your decision," said Davis. "You can be an awful nuisance, Maclain, when you hook yourself on a fixed idea and start gumming up the law." He sat down in a chair across the desk and toasted his own good will with two hardy swallows.

"Damn it," he muttered as he tried to pull the chair up closer, "I always forget that the furniture in here is fastened to the floor."

"I always know where it is when it's fastened down," said Duncan Maclain. "I've only had a few secondhand facts on the Jordan case. Suppose you tell me more."

Archer's teeth clicked as he bit the end from a cigar.

"He'll tell you all right, Captain. You can stop him if you've heard it before."

"Yes," said Davis, "it's the old one about the little girl who worked day and night and made good in the city. I hope I won't be a bore."

"Don't be whimsical," said Maclain. "You have a Peter Pannish quality about you, Larry, when you get cocksure."

"This time I'm right," said Davis crisply. "The Singleton girl had milked him plenty—fifty thousand dollars or more—and on the top of that she was planning to break up his marriage. You should know that yourself. She blew into that cocktail party uninvited while you were there the day before."

"Remind me to tell you something," interrupted Maclain.

"What?" Davis asked with quick suspicion.

"About her voice." The Captain snuffed out his cigarette. "I'll tell you when you're finished. Right now I want to hear more."

"I'll bet a dollar," mumbled Archer, that he's going to tell us the Singleton dame could sing."

Davis said, "There's plenty more. She showed up at the apartment yesterday afternoon about half past five. The timing was as perfect as a billiard shot. It was the houseman's day off. Jordan even sent his secretary out to make sure there was nobody in."

"Lucia Jordan told me she and Bob Morse were having cocktails in a near-by bar," the Captain inserted gently.

"Now what the hell has that got to do with it?"

"I was merely thinking," Maclain said ruminatively, "that in planning this carefully thought out murder Larmar didn't know exactly what time his wife and Morse might drop in."

"Carefully thought out, hell," said Davis. "There are moments, Maclain, when you vaccinate my innermost skin. Troy Singleton came up there to put the bite on him for more money, maybe to tell him that she was pregnant or something, and that he'd better throw Lucia out and move her in."

"Was she wearing a shawl?" the Captain asked with a grin.

"She was wearing a dress trimmed with bunnies," said Archer, "and the weather was hotter than blistering sin."

"Quit interrupting me every time I start," the inspector protested. "Jordan knew this dame was coming. He mixed a couple of drinks."

"To drink to his allegedly promised son and heir," the Captain muttered under his breath.

Davis ignored him. "While he was mixing them, they started to argue. Troy was in the study, Larmar in the bar. The argument got worse. She slapped his face and he dropped the cocktail tray as he was carrying it in. The girl ran out on the terrace and sat down in the chair in front of his desk. Jordan went into the gun room and got a pistol."

"I hope to tell you," said Archer. "It had a barrel as long as a ballet dancer's shin. He calmly walked out there and let her have it, just as those bells across the street began to ring."

"And what kind of a pistol," asked Duncan Maclain, "has a barrel as long as a ballet dancer's shin?"

"It's a target pistol, according to the ballistics department," Davis explained. "A single-shot, nine-millimeter German gun called a Buchel."

The Captain reached up with his fingers and began to twist a lock of crisp dark hair.

"That gun has a set trigger, Davis. I've shot one myself."

The inspector smoothed his close-cropped mustache and admitted, "Well, it does go off pretty easy."

"Pretty easy?" said Archer. "I saw it tested in the laboratory this morning. It'll go off if you stroke it with a hair. But first you have to cock it by pressing a lever on the side."

"It did the job," said Davis. "It's peculiar what murderers do. Jordan started to wipe off his fingerprints with a handkerchief, and then remembered that he could always say he handled the gun in the gun room and his prints would naturally be there. Then he decided to get rid of the gun by tossing it over the wall, only to realize it was bound to be found. Finally he hid it in the bushes along with his handkerchief. That's where Archer found it."

"And what about the body, Inspector?"

"He had a story about that too, as most of them do. He claims he didn't shoot her and got panicky because no one else was there. All he could think of was that he had to get her off the terrace. So he took her into the gun room and put her on newspapers, intending to burn them later if they got bloody. She has an apartment uptown. Somehow or other, Jordan hoped to get her out of this place and up there. The only trouble was that this Mrs. Oliver who lives above him heard the shot and gave us a call." He paused and glared ineffectually. "Well, what do you think of it now?"

"There are a couple of questions I'd like to ask." The Captain quit twisting his hair. "You say the girl got mad after this quarrel and ran out on the terrace and sat down. Then Jordan came out and shot her."

"She lit a cigarette," Davis told him, "took one puff and put it down on an ash tray. It went out against the glass. We found it and a burned match from her bag in an ash tray on the desk to the right of her chair."

"You asked me what I thought about it," the Captain said. "I'll tell you. I don't think Jordan killed her. He's a gun crank. He wouldn't take a cocked hair trigger pistol and carry it out on that terrace to shoot a girl. The chances are a hundred to one the gun would go off before he got to his desk. He certainly wouldn't use a single-shot gun that cocks by depressing a lever on the side. That sounds clumsy as hell. What would the girl be doing in the meantime?"

Davis stood up. "You can do what you damn well please,

Captain. He murdered her and I'll send him to the electric chair."

"I promised to tell you about her voice," Maclain continued with unruffled smoothness. "It was well trained and had a great carrying quality. I heard her talking to Jordan out on the terrace. She didn't come to that cocktail party without an invitation. Somebody wrote her a letter on Jordan's private stationery, Davis. It might pay you to find out who invited her there."

". . . if it be not to come,"

I

D E QUINCEY, viewing murder as a fine art, took delight in propounding the thesis that a first class killing had certain basic elements which made it a thing of beauty and a joy forever. He wrote, of course, from the untouched heights of a grinning and satirical point of view. It is doubtful that his volume would have reached the printer's hand had his mother expired violently via the bashed-in-head-and-mallet route, or had De Quincey himself discovered a corpse in his study chair.

The newly born murder, before it attains ripe maturity and dies a natural death of public ennui, has many things to do; not the least among them is shockingly changing the lives of all those immediately concerned, and at the same time reaching out haphazardly to daub a dozen others more remotely connected with its dripping brush of tar.

The death of Troy Singleton was no exception.

A book had been abandoned, along with a profile of its author. The editor of a national publication, expecting a Jordan serial, had hurriedly changed his schedule. A household was closed and its personal effects temporarily abandoned to the impersonal scrutiny of photographers and other representatives of the law, who charted, swept, molded and searched until every piece of furniture, selected so carefully by Lucia, and every inch of the rooms and terrace had been reduced to a scale of metrical measure.

Even Winnie, the cocker spaniel, was affected. Like his master, Larmar Jordan, his life of luxury suddenly ceased. He found himself banished to a kennel, to move about whimpering uneasily in the confines of some veterinary's cell.

Lucia too had left her home. New York was unusually overcrowded and the management, arrogant with the flush of abnormal business, refused to allow dogs in the only accommodations she could obtain in a near-by hotel.

The grinning ribs of what once had been the Jordan home were left to the care of Harry, the houseman, and Paul.

In the apartment above, Mrs. Evelyn Oliver, a conservative widow of fifty, addicted to Proust, the collection of china dogs, and the herringbone stitch in knitting sweaters, found herself unexpectedly rocketed into a brief but blazing notoriety. Over a lean period of years, men had studiedly passed Mrs. Oliver by. Now in a few brief hours, she had talked to so many that their identity had not only become confused but she had lost track entirely of what she had said. Given two more days of reporters, it would not have surprised Mrs. Oliver to find that she herself had discovered Troy Singleton's body weltering in blood in her bathtub.

Nevertheless, when her door bell rang in the middle of the afternoon, she was somewhat surprised at the announcement of Carrie, her colored maid, that a blind man was waiting outside in the hall.

"Don't be silly, Carrie." Mrs. Oliver put her knitting down. "I don't know any blind men."

"No'm." Carrie rolled her expressive eyes. The last couple of days had indeed been a circus. "This one says he hates to disturb you but could you talk with him."

"What's his name?"

"He's a Captain, or sumpin'."

"Didn't you get his name?"

"I didn't hear so well, Mrs. Oliver. He's got a dog with a handle on it."

"A handle? Carrie, you're talking silly." Mrs. Oliver wrinkled her placid brow.

"You'll see," said Carrie, shaking her head portentously. "Maybe he carries that dog around with him."

"Well, let him in, and don't stand here chattering."

Carrie started for the door.

Mrs. Oliver said, "Wait! Are you certain he's blind?" She glanced down modestly at her voluminous negligee.

"Yas'm," Carrie insisted. "Ain't no need to put nothin' on with him. He can't see nothin' at all."

Mrs. Oliver picked up her knitting and put it down again. Carrie was a little fresh, but it was her own fault. She'd always been too lenient with servants.

She stood rather tremulously as the man and the dog came in.

"I'm Captain Duncan Maclain, Mrs. Oliver. I'm a friend of Mr. and Mrs. Jordan's." He held out his hand and smiled, and for the briefest instant she had a sensation that his well-formed eyes were looking straight through her.

Embarrassment seized her. She had expected to be shocked but the only thing unusual about the tall straight man who stood facing her was the striking quality of his ease and charm, and the excellent cut and fit of his light gray suit.

Her embarrassment vanished when she shook his hand. Instinctively she realized that Carrie's statement about his blindness might be true, but that somehow this handsome stranger would always manage to get along.

She was about to ask him to sit down when it occurred to her that there might be some special etiquette in offering a blind man a chair. He saved her the necessity by seating himself comfortably without fumbling. It took her a moment to recognize that the self-sufficient German shepherd by his side had guided him imperceptibly toward the divan.

"Do you mind if I smoke?" he asked. "It helps me to think."

"Not at all." Mrs. Oliver resumed her knitting. She wasn't at all sure of the purpose of his visit, but a pleasant sense of flattery had enveloped her in arousing the interest of this debonair man. It was exciting to watch him flash his lighter and locate the precise spot where the tip of the cigarette met the steady flame. It was fascinating to see him locate the onyx ash tray on the table beside him by searching gently with a quick sure movement of his sentient hand.

"You must be a very patient woman, Mrs. Oliver," he remarked, drawing his cigarette into a glow. "You seem to have had a lot of callers during the day."

"Dear me, I don't mind." She looked up from her work. "At my age, life's apt to become dull and callers are welcome." Her fingers grew busy again and her face sobered. "I hope the manager hasn't complained."

"The manager?" asked Maclain.

"You mentioned the callers. Well, there have been a lot, one after another. I thought maybe he told you so."

The Captain's expressive mouth moved in a line of sympathy. He shook his head. "I haven't even talked to the manager, Mrs. Oliver. But I happen to have been mixed up unofficially in a lot of police investigations. Besides that, callers leave traces after they go."

"Traces?" She dropped a stitch, looking around the orderly room.

The Captain smiled as though he had seen her puzzled expression.

"Traces in the air," he explained, and waved one hand in a quick expressive arc. "Your voice informs me that you are a very charming lady. I happen to know that you live here alone. I doubt very much that during the day you've tried out three different mixtures of very fragrant pipe tobacco and topped it off with one very strong cigar."

Mrs. Oliver picked up her stitch and said, "Gracious me!"

The Captain laughed. "And now that I've demonstrated my own great cleverness, I'll tell you why I came."

"Well, it is clever," Mrs. Oliver insisted. "Imagine smelling all those things in my apartment. It certainly would never have occurred to me."

"And yet," said Maclain, "I understand that you're a woman who's very observing. Most people aren't, you know. The courts find every day that out of a crowd which witnesses an accident there's scarcely a person who remembers anything."

Mrs. Oliver set her lips. "I remember most things, that is, things that I actually see."

"I'm sure you do," said Duncan Maclain. "That's why I came here. Mr. Jordan's under arrest for murder."

"And quite right too," said Mrs. Oliver firmly.

"If he's guilty, I agree." The Captain pursed his lips. "But the actual firing of that shot by Larmar Jordan happens to be one of the things you didn't see. Or is it?" The Captain leaned forward suddenly and let the smoke of his cigarette curl up about the intentness of his face.

"I saw her slumped down in the chair." Mrs. Oliver's needles clicked on merrily.

"But you're quite sure Larmar wasn't standing there in front of her?"

"There was nobody there."

The Captain put out his cigarette, crossed his long legs and locked his hands about one knee.

"I'm sure you want to see justice done, Mrs. Oliver. I haven't any eyes and I have to draw pictures in my brain, pictures that are made through movements. A girl's been killed and a man is facing the electric chair. If I stand up now, will you go to the trouble of leading me to the spot where you were when you heard that shot and then showing me exactly what you did, and describing to me in detail exactly what you were able to see?"

"I don't understand what good it'll do, but I'll do it." Mrs. Oliver relinquished her knitting and stood up.

Up until now, the entire affair had been a bit of a lark. Holding onto this blind man's hand and re-living events of twenty-four hours before, she felt disconcerted, as though she herself had unwittingly become an integral part of this tragedy.

She led the Captain into another room and put his hand on the back of a chair.

"I was seated right here," she told him in a voice approaching a whisper. "Carrie, my maid, was out—it was her afternoon off—and I'd fixed myself a cup of tea. The windows in the sitting room were open, as they are right now. I'd just sat down when the chimes began to ring. I remember now I was adding sugar to my tea. I like to hear the chimes—they play hymns that are always a great comfort to me. Then I heard the shot."

"Did you recognize the hymn?" asked Duncan Maclain.

"That's a funny think to ask," said Mrs. Oliver, "because I play a sort of game with the carillon, trying to recognize what it's going to play from the first few notes. The shot must have upset me because I didn't recognize it until I ran into the other room to look out of the window. I should have, too. The first four notes should have told me that it's an old favorite of mine, *Abide With Me.*"

"Yes," said Maclain. "You should have known it. That must mean that the shot came instantly. You say that you ran to the window?"

"Yes." She led him through the living room and stopped him at the window sill. "The girl was in that chair there." Mrs. Oliver had pointed before she remembered that the Captain couldn't see. She went into a description. "There's an awning across the other end of the terrace. Larmar Jordan's desk is under the awning. He sits there in a swivel chair working every afternoon. I've watched him often. Sometimes he looks up but usually he's so engrossed that I don't believe he has ever seen me."

"There's a green privet hedge back of his desk, isn't there?" the Captain asked.

"Yes, and on each side of the terrace, too."

"How far is that hedge in back of his chair, Mrs. Oliver?"

She measured with a seamstress' eye. "Not very far. A couple of feet perhaps. Maybe three. The girl was sitting slumped down in a white metal chair across the desk from Mr. Jordan's. She had her back to me."

The Captain whirled on her quickly. "You told the police that you saw her slump down, Mrs. Oliver." His voice was edged. "Did she change her position after you got to this window, or didn't she?"

She thought a long time. "I can't remember," she said unsteadily.

"Do you want me to think that you're equally forgetful about seeing some one escape from that terrace, Mrs. Oliver?"

"There was no one there." Her voice had grown firm again. "I'd have told the police if I'd seen anyone. What difference could it possibly make to me?"

"It could have landed you in jail as a material witness," said Duncan Maclain. "Jail, Mrs. Oliver, is a most unpleasant place to be." He had turned to face the terrace again as though picturing something he could never really see.

"There was no one there, nothing but the girl and his chair. You have to believe me." She clutched his elbow pleadingly.

"But you still can't remember whether Troy Singleton moved or not after you saw her." His blind eyes stared out stonily.

"What difference can that make, Captain Maclain? She was quite dead, wasn't she?"

"It can mean a man's life," said Duncan Maclain. "If Larmar Jordan's story is true, he was standing in the study down below us when he saw that girl slump down in the chair. If that was before you got from your dining-room chair to this window, he wouldn't have had time to leave the terrace. He couldn't have shot her possibly."

2

Lucia Jordan had a headache. She got up from an ineffectual attempt to sleep it off and stared with distaste at the unimaginative furnishings of her room.

It was after six, but the end of the day had merely made the afternoon more muggy and depressingly warm.

Lucia was moving in a vacuum where nothing functioned normally. She had found coherent thought impossible in the blighted Arday apartment. Too many memories clung to her surroundings. Now she found that coherent thought was equally impossible even in the impersonal environment of the big hotel. There was no escape from the touch of murder.

She lit a cigarette, found that it made her headache worse, and put it out again.

Her windows opened on a court. She stared out and up at a square patch of sky which was turning gray, holding a hint of rain. She drew the shades and lit the lights by her bureau. It felt better to be closed in. The windows across the court had taken on a malignant quality, as though unseen guests behind them might be watching.

Mrs. Lucia Jordan had become an object of interest. Lucia Jordan, society matron and beautiful wife of the arrested author, Larmar. Lucia Jordan, the perfect wife, perfect hostess. Thank God, the newspapers hadn't been able to label her "perfect mother." At least there weren't any children for them to dip in their filthy pool.

She showered and dressed, choosing something quiet and cool.

It was strange how one got used to a man over a period of years. Life with a husband knit itself about you with thousands of tiny stitches. Its encompassing shape shielded you against the coldness of the world. There should be some way of discovering that its snug-fitting warmth was pleasant and homey before all the stitches unraveled completely, and the garment of marriage was irretrievably gone.

One must eat, she supposed, because it was a habit. It shocked her to realize that for the first evening in many months she wanted to have dinner with Larmar.

There was a time when she had appreciated the way he ordered, and admired his knowledge of food and wines with a touch of girlish awe.

There was a time when sitting in the dark seclusion of a movie with him, she'd liked to hold his hand.

Something horrible had happened to her marriage with Larmar.

Self-recrimination was a weakling's refuge but Lucia began to wonder just how responsible she had been personally in the deliberate shooting of Troy.

She'd talked to Larmar that afternoon in jail. It was coldly sobering to sit across from your husband at a plain board table and hear him saying, "I've been a bit of an ass, darling, maybe because I thought you'd grown tired of me, but I'm not a big enough ass to shoot a woman. All I needed to do was to run out of money to get rid of Troy."

The sun had crept down to shine through the small square window and fall across the table where it left the shadow of a single bar.

She'd tried to tell him that she hadn't grown tired, but merely careless. She'd assured him with genuine tears in her eyes that she didn't believe him guilty.

"You seem to be a minority of one, darling."

He received her protestations with a cynical grin. She knew he was thinking that at the time of Troy's murder she and Bob Morse were having cocktails together in Robertina's bar.

The telephone rang.

Sarah Hanley was on the wire, more precise and brittle than usual, her throaty voice laced with unobtrusive sympathy. "Just because the police make a silly mistake, Lucia, you don't need to run away and hide from everyone. I had an awful time worming out the name of your hotel from Paul."

"I want to hide out," Lucia told her tersely. "I'm sick of people staring at me."

"Well, you'll help Larmar more by appearing in public," Sarah announced in her most matter-of-fact business manner. "Public opinion's a powerful thing, Lucia. I happen to deal with it in my business as a literary agent. If you want the world to think that Larmar's guilty, the best way that you can do it is to crawl off into some hole."

"All right," Lucia said dispiritedly. "What do you want me to do?"

"Eat dinner with me at the Pheasant on University Place." She cut Lucia's protest short with, "I'm waiting downstairs now. That lawyer, Jess Ferguson, is expensive and you'll need money. to fight this thing. There're some angles about Larmar's work that I have to talk over with you."

"Paul knows more about it than I do."

"I'm waiting downstairs." Sarah Hanley hung up the phone.

"Damn the woman," said Lucia, but unaccountably she felt a little better. There was something reassuring about Sarah Hanley's unexcited, cold commercial tone.

She powdered her nose and went down.

The lobby was packed with a milling dinner throng, and at first she couldn't locate Sarah. Her nerves strung to a point of breaking had made her supersensitive to anyone's regard or she might never have become conscious of the man with the deep cleft chin.

He was wearing an ill-cut heavy double-breasted suit of blue that stretched so tight across his shoulders the coat seemed too small. His eyes were brown and calculatingly cold. The cleft in his chin made him noticeable if nothing else, for it was cut so deep that it might have been the remnant of some disfiguring scar.

From his seat on a high-backed red plush divan, he looked up from a newspaper spread across his knees to study Lucia with a frank unfriendly stare.

Without warning, he got up and left the lobby through a side door.

He might have been any casual guest in the big hotel except that he left his paper, indicating that he'd read it through. Lucia had a distinct impression that he'd been seated in the lobby for a long time, watching the elevators and checking to see who entered and left every car.

She finally located Sarah near the front door. Face to face with Lucia, the agent lost some of her aplomb, merely guiding Lucia out of the hotel with a sympathetic touch on her arm.

They walked to University Place in silence, but Sarah insisted on cocktails after they sat down.

The drink restored some of Lucia's lost animation. Taking advantage of Lucia's returning color, Sarah chattered vivaciously throughout the meal. Not until coffee was on the table did she mention Larmar. Then it was to ask, "Do you think Larmar could continue his book in—the present circumstances?"

Lucia stirred her coffee and said, "Why don't you say in jail? Everyone else does."

"I thought it might help him to forget himself, Lucia."

"Of course. Then there's the question of money too, which you mentioned over the phone." Lucia sounded a little bitter.

"One has to be practical in these things," Sarah reminded her. "I understand from Paul that Larmar's affairs aren't in the best of order." She surveyed Lucia thoughtfully over the edge of her cup. "The apartment rent's going on. You have additional expenses of a hotel. There's Ferguson to be paid, and Paul and Harry. Unless you have some money of your own, Lucia, you may be facing a problem of just what to do."

"You're Larmar's agent. I'll leave the practicality to you." Lucia rubbed her temples with her finger tips, beginning to feel the return of the afternoon's pain.

Sarah put her coffee cup down. "I understand you've retained Captain Duncan Maclain."

"I felt it was the least I could do."

"He may be expensive."

"I didn't ask him." Lucia's blue eyes were antagonistic. "Is anything too expensive to put Larmar back in circulation again?"

"Of course not," Sarah hastily agreed. She looked at her diamond wrist watch and signaled their waitress for the check. "Can you stand going up to the apartment this evening?"

"Why?"

"Paul asked me to find out if you'd come. It's after eight now, and I have an appointment uptown."

"What does Paul want with me?"

"He thinks as I do," Sarah Hanley said as she paid the check. "We believe that you can do more than either of us to keep Larmar busy with his book. Besides that, Paul's expecting Captain Maclain."

"All right, I'll go. I'm getting so I can stand anything, even the unspoken sympathy of doormen and elevator boys."

"Good!" Sarah stood up in her usual brusque manner. "I'll walk up to Tenth Street with you and take a Fifth Avenue bus uptown."

She started on her stock line of endless chatter and continued it until she parted with Lucia at the entrance to the Arday Apartments. There she took Lucia's hand and said gravely, "For once in my life, I'm not concerned with commissions, Lucia. I'm fond of you both. Do what you can to get Larmar working down there."

She bustled off, leaving Lucia standing under the canopy.

The doorman restored some of her self-confidence by saying "Good evening, Mrs. Jordan," with just the right inflection and not a hint of strain. But the elevator boy was frankly bursting with suppressed curiosity. He stopped at the fourteenth floor with a flourish and Lucia could feel his eyes at her back as she walked down the hall.

Maclain greeted her as she opened the door. It was a relief to take sanctuary in the familiar study. The Captain's tranquilly excited manner calmed her headache with the efficiency of a powerful sedative.

His mood had changed since her visit to his office that morning. Then he had been close to apathetic. Now, Lucia felt, his well-controlled air of triumph had some new found information that offered a line of action. Had she known him better she might have been less encouraged. Action itself was a stimulant to Duncan Maclain, causing every one of his highly trained senses virtually to boil.

Schnucke stood up as they entered the study and stuck close to the Captain's left side until he and Lucia sat down.

Voices came from the gun room. Lucia must have started and drawn in her breath for Maclain said quickly, "That's Brownie and Paul."

"Oh." She took out her vanity case to regain composure. It was only yesterday that the police had forced Larmar to open that gun room. It was an incident in her life that Lucia didn't want to recall.

The Captain seemed to understand. "I asked Brownie to come here, Lucia. I wanted some expert advice on guns and Brownie's thoroughly familiar with Larmar's collection."

"You mean I may have to sell them?" She was glad it had

grown dark outside. Morbid fascination kept drawing her attention to the terrace doors.

"Larmar already had that idea in mind," the Captain told her. "I got that from Paul. But Brownie's dead against it. He says that it might be sold off piece by piece, but as a collection it wouldn't bring a tenth of its value. Too much income tax and war. However, that isn't what I wanted to know. I wanted information on the pistol that killed Troy."

A flame leaped up inside her. "You're going to prove it wasn't Larmar's gun?"

"The police have already proved it was," said Duncan Maclain. He lowered his voice. "I'm working on an idea so crazy that I hesitate even to confide in you. I talked to Mrs. Oliver upstairs this afternoon. She ran to her window within seconds after that shot was fired. I'm convinced that she saw no one leave the terrace—because there was no one there."

"But somebody shot her, Captain." Lucia found her throat was harsh and dry. "Who was it—if it wasn't Larmar?"

"A man in a tower across the street," said Duncan Maclain. "I hope to prove, with Brownie's help, that Troy was killed by the man who plays the carillon."

3

Bob Morse dropped in shortly after nine. His friendship with the Jordans and his opportune arrival at the scene had automatically pushed him into covering the story of the Singleton shooting for the conservative *Globe-Tribune*.

Bob had always hated murder stories. During many years of newspaper work he had managed to conceal a disturbing streak of sentiment under a slowly growing layer of fat and a carefully cultivated brittleness of manner. He knew that his susceptibility toward other people's troubles had been a definite handicap in his newspaper career. It was the job of a good reporter to dig up the unadorned facts and present them to the public unvarnished by that reporter's personal dislikes or sympathies. Morse was constantly getting involved with white-haired mothers, destitute wives and little children with rickets, and turning in sob sister stories.

Experience had taught him that three quarts of Bourbon were a helpful reminder of the fact that breaking hearts were the bane of the city editor and that the public wanted to read about love nests and not be reminded of the hour that dear daddy was scheduled for a hot squat in the electric chair.

The whole thing was most discouraging. It had finally driven him to the social suicide of profiles, where the friendship of important figures could be alienated by subtly laying their soft spots bare.

Bob knew that the tabloids would gleefully tear the Jordans to pieces. Consequently, his story for the *Globe-Tribune* was handled with thoughtful care. Lucia had read it that morning before she consulted Duncan Maclain. She was full of appreciation for the sensitive and understanding way in which Bob had covered her married life with Larmar, yet when he arrived at the apartment she simply said, "Thanks, Bob. Will you have a drink?"

"Not tonight, Lucia." He sank down in a chair, his round face serene with an inner glow at his own unusual abstinence. He looked from her to Paul Hirst. "What's new? Did either of you talk to Larmar today?"

"I did, Bob. I had dinner with Sarah Hanley tonight, too."

"Humph," Bob grunted morosely. "She'll want ten per cent of the lawyer's fee."

"Sarah's not so bad. Why do you dislike her so?"

"It's her type." His pudgy fingers drummed on the arm of the chair. "She's one of those dames who's so damned efficient she irritates me."

"There're times when she makes a lot of sense," said Paul. "She wants Larmar to go on with his book."

"Paul and I were just discussing it."

"I told you so." Bob held up ten fingers and traced an invisible per cent mark in the air.

Lucia said, "That's not entirely true. We will need the money and nobody else seems to care. At Sybella Ford's suggestion, I retained Captain Maclain today."

"Maclain? Well, I'll be damned." Bob hitched himself forward in the chair. "Can I use that? He and his dogs are good copy. What's he working on?"

Lucia started to say what the Captain had told her and changed her mind. "You'd better ask him yourself, Bob." She pointed toward the gun room. "He and Brownie are in there."

"I'll take a look." Bob left and crossed the foyer to lean against the door of the gun room.

The Captain was seated on the table, threading the length of a peculiar looking whip through one hand. Brownie in a chair beside him was concentrating on a long-barreled pistol which fitted neatly into a polished wooden box lined with green velvet.

Maclain said, without turning his head, "I was wondering when I got mixed up in this how long it would be before the gentlemen of the press arrived. Come in, Mr. Morse, and sit down."

"I'm not a gentleman." Bob took a chair at the end of the table and blinked at Maclain. "I'm practically a member of the family. Furthermore, I haven't been drinking. How did you know it was me? Unless the memory of our last conversation is a blank, I have an idea you should associate my presence with an odor of imported gin."

"With footstep light as floating thistledown," Maclain said softly, "and a hand upon my shoulder, soft as drifting flakes of snow."

"That quotation's as phony as a harlot's kiss." Morse widened his round eyes. "What's it supposed to be from?"

"It should be from Chaucer's *Faerie Queene,*" the Captain told him soberly, "but it happens to be a figment of my poetical mind, engendered by the way you leaned on me on that sofa day before yesterday. The operation nearly caved me in."

Bob sighed. "So my footfalls betray me, and Spenser had a copyright on that particular Queene when I went to school. I've been telling myself for years, 'Look, Pig's Knuckle, it's time for your dieting to begin!'" He leaned closer to examine the long-barreled gun and asked, "What the hell do you call that thing?"

"It's a lace tree whip from Jamaica," Maclain said, holding up the object in his hand. "It's all in one piece, made out of fiber from which the bark has been removed. Look at the butt. It feels like several layers of woven cloth to my fingers, but it's still all part of the tree."

"Awkward to shoot a dame with, I'd say."

The Captain's eyebrows moved upward in an interested wriggle. "Oh, I take it you're referring to the gun."

Bob said dryly, "Yeah. Is that the one?"

"Scarcely," Brownie put in. "The one, as you call it, is down at police headquarters tagged Exhibit A, but this is very much like it."

Bob took it gingerly from the case and examined it with the barrel pointing toward the floor.

"It's not loaded," said Brownie.

"I've covered enough accidental shootings," Bob told him, "to have heard that one before." He restored the pistol to its velvet box. "Is that part of Larmar's collection?"

"Well, not exactly," Brownie explained. "This is a Stotzer Perfekt Pistole. Larmar used this and the other one in target matches." He picked the gun from its box again, holding it easily. "This is a twenty-two. Most target pistols are twenty-twos, but the gun which killed the girl was a Buchel which Larmar had had specially made. It was a nine millimeter, a larger bore."

"I want you to take a look at the trigger, Mr. Morse," said Maclain. "You'll notice there're two. Show him, Brownie."

The gunsmith made a quick skilled movement of his hands and said, "I showed the Captain this just before you came in. I've cocked this gun. Now I'll pull the rear trigger down."

Morse leaned still closer, listening intently for the click of the hammer fall. Finally he said, "What happened? Has it gone off?"

"The rear trigger doesn't fire it," Brownie explained. "When I pull it, it merely sets the front one." He held the empty pistol out from him, pointing at a spot on the wall, and continued, "This is a real hair trigger gun with an extremely heavy mainspring and an extremely short hammer fall. It takes a lot of practice to learn to shoot one. You see, I put my index finger very carefully on the edge of this front trigger, but I'm pushing away from it instead of pulling. Now, all I need to do is relax the muscles of my hand."

Bob heard the click of the hammer fall. "It strikes me," said Morse, "that that would be a dangerous gun to have around."

Brownie smiled. "Target shooters say that you 'wish the trigger off' instead of pulling it, but I've seen them set even finer than this, so fine that just by blowing on it you could discharge the gun."

"Try it yourself, Mr. Morse," said Duncan Maclain.

Bob went through the motions with Brownie guiding his hand. Before he got the gun into position and almost without realizing that he'd touched the trigger, he heard the hammer fall."

"You'd have put a bullet through the Captain's leg," said Brownie, taking the gun.

Maclain put down the whip and left his place on the table. He seemed to have lost interest entirely in Brownie's demonstration. The two men watched him with growing bewilderment as he made a long silent tour of the gun room, opening cases and haphazardly picking up weapon after weapon to handle it briefly. Each one was returned to its place with a nicety which Bob Morse found almost unbelievable, although he was watching every movement of the Captain's accurate arm.

After a while he quit the guns and turned his attention to a panel of swords and daggers hung on the wall. He lifted several down, pulling them half from their scabbards and feeling their blades, running his finger along the metal with the delicate touch of an expert carver.

Six of the swords and a couple of daggers seemed to satisfy him. He returned to his perch on the table and said abruptly, "The police found a forty-five automatic in the drawer of this table, Brownie. Larmar had a permit for it, but the gun was unloaded. Did he have any ammunition?"

"Plenty, I believe," said Brownie. "He used that gun for target shooting too, but he bought several hundred rounds of ammunition from my shop just before the war."

Brownie got up and went to a built-in cabinet in the corner.

"He keeps his ammunition in here, but it's locked. Wait a minute, and I'll get the key from Paul." He went out into the study.

Maclain said to Bob, "You can help me, if you will. I'm working on a crazy idea."

"Yeah, I get it. I'm supposed to bottle up the story about you being on the case."

"I may be so wrong that any mention of it in the press might prejudice the public, and a jury, against Larmar."

"I'll keep my mouth shut," said Bob, "but I want first look-in when the bars are down."

"And I need more help than that." Maclain turned halfway as though he might see the man at the end of the table. "My partner, Spud Savage, is in Washington with Army Intelligence. I need somebody to dig up every fact I can get about that girl called Troy."

"What about the police?"

"They'll tell you things they won't tell me," said Duncan Maclain. "We're worrying a bone from different ends, Bob. I'm trying to set Larmar free."

"I'll give you a profile of her," said Bob. "You can count on me."

Brownie came back with the key and opened the cabinet. "He has plenty of ammunition," he announced after a moment's search. "Forty-fives, nine millimeters, and twenty-twos. Ammunition's been hard to get since the war."

Maclain said, "You've been around guns most of your life, Brownie, haven't you?"

Brownie's soft gray eyes were reminiscent. "I started shooting a pop gun when I was two. My first collection was cap pistols when I was ten. I must have had twenty or more."

"Then tell me something." The Captain thoughtfully clasped

his restless fingers. "If you were bent on killing someone with a single shot, why would you use a nine-millimeter pistol, Brownie, instead of a twenty-two?"

"That's not difficult to answer." Brownie locked the cabinet and sat down. "Without getting into ballistics, the nine-milli-meter bullet's bigger, more powerful and more deadly. It will crush bone and kill, where you might only get a wound with a twenty-two."

Bob said, "That's interesting, except that it makes me slightly ill." He looked down at Schnucke and asked, "Which dog is that? The Seeing-Eye one or the one that's as dangerous as a loaded gun? I've heard tell that on some of your cases you have a trick of changing them around."

"It's a trick that I keep to myself," said Duncan Maclain, and brought back the subject with a smile. "I want to go a step further. The forty-five caliber has even more crushing power than the nine millimeter. As a single shot weapon of murder, for the reasons you've just given me wouldn't it be still more likely to appeal to you?"

Brownie closed the box on the Stotzer and put it away. When he returned to the table he stood leaning on the edge for a few seconds, staring at Maclain. "I think you've got something, Captain," he said after a while. "Larmar had a forty-five with ammunition. He had a tricky Buchel with ammunition, but he kept the ammunition for both of them locked up in that closet in the corner. He had to get it out of there to load either gun. He's one of the best amateur pistol shots I know. You want to find out why he used that tricky Buchel instead of the forty-five to kill the girl."

The Captain nodded silently.

Brownie wet his lips and said, "He didn't, if you're asking me."

4

Brownie and Bob Morse departed around ten, leaving Maclain in the study with Lucia and Paul.

Lucia found herself harassed by a sense of the fantastic. It was contributed to in no little part by the Captain's blindness plus an underlying air of abstraction which had wrapped itself about Maclain. He chatted easily with her and Paul, drawing her out about her visit to Larmar and Sarah Hanley's suggestion that even though Larmar was incarcerated his work go on.

To Lucia, the police had been real and frighteningly efficient, driving straight through along a predetermined line. Duncan Maclain, as a guest in her home, had been a figure of interest, fascinating to watch and thrilling to talk to due to his exciting knowledge of so many subjects off the beaten track. Tonight, with Larmar's fate and her own future dependent on his astuteness, she found herself worried. An element of unreality had settled down on Paul and herself and the familiar apartment.

The focal point of this disconcerting sensation was Captain Duncan Maclain. His inconsistency upset her; not an inconsistency of movement, for he sat quite still, his long legs stretched before him, but an inconsistency of thought.

She was hungry for comforting assurance. The Captain kept hopping about conversationally, giving out nothing and swallowing disconnected items about Harry, the houseman, Sarah Hanley, Larmar's early childhood, and Winnie, the cocker. Each item went down with a movement of his throat, as a man might take a pill.

He became an arabesque to Lucia as the evening wore on. Blind man and dog merged together in a flat intricate pattern of the renaissance, combining animal and human without background or perspective. After a while the arabesque absorbed herself and Paul, making them also a part of the pattern, and just as unreal.

"The collection belonged to Larmar's father?"

"Yes."

"Harry's off on Thursday afternoons?"

"Yes."

"He doesn't sleep in?"

"No."

"Tell me something about literary agents, Lucia. Would there be any chance of Sarah Hanley making a sale that Larmar wouldn't know about?"

"I doubt it." That answer was from Paul.

"Maybe I'd better talk to her myself. How long have you lived here?"

"Four years now."

"Do they play the carillon every afternoon?"

"At quarter of six."

"And at quarter to eleven on Sundays," put in Paul. "After a bad night when Larmar wanted to sleep late, he used to cuss it blue."

"The police have a note written to Troy Singleton inviting her to your cocktail party. They found it in Larmar's desk. Do you know anything about it, Lucia?"

"He showed it to me and accused me of writing it. I didn't." She'd never realized how difficult it was to think when you couldn't see any expression in the eyes of the man you were talking to.

"Can Larmar type, Paul?"

"He's fast with two fingers, but he hasn't used the machine in a long time."

"Did he ever dictate such a note to you?"

"Never."

"Do you think he wrote it himself?"

"Search me," said Paul. "He's unpredictable in a lot of things. It's hard to tell what he'll do."

Maclain got up with the easy lift of a man in perfect trim. "I want to take a turn about the terrace and get it clear in my mind."

"It's dark out there," said Lucia, her thoughts far away.

"It's never dark to me," said Duncan Maclain. Paul stood up and the Captain added, "You don't need to bother. I'll come back when I'm through." He disappeared onto the terrace.

Lucia wanted to ask Paul a question, but Paul was stroking his black mustache and staring curiously out through the terrace door. Lucia didn't want to look out there, yet an impelling desire to check on the Captain's movements forced her to turn her head.

Schnucke was still on the floor, kept inert by some unseen signal of Maclain's quick hand as he left his chair. The shepherd lay head on paws, her dark eyes fixed unmovingly on the spot outside of the terrace doors where the light from the study made a square.

Lucia said, "How does he know what he's doing, Paul? What does he hope to find out there?"

Maclain crossed the terrace appearing briefly in the light from the door.

"He counts his steps," Paul told her, "and apparently never forgets them. He can move with perfect confidence around any place where he's been before."

Lucia said, "What does he hope to find out there?" and listened. But the terrace had swallowed Maclain in quiet.

Paul said, "He can't see anything if he finds it," and added as an afterthought, "You can search me. I can't even imagine what a blind man would be looking for."

They sat silent for a long time.

Lucia swung about startled as her bedroom door opened and the Captain stepped out into the study, holding blackened hands before him. "It's getting late," he said without preamble. "May I wash up before I go?"

"Sure," said Paul. "Come along." He got up and took the Captain's arm.

"What did you find?" asked Lucia.

Maclain turned away from his escort as though he'd forgotten about her and said absentmindedly, "I don't know. I came in through your room."

She watched his straight figure disappear into the foyer headed for Paul's bedroom. Striding along beside the secretary, he looked abnormally tall.

A breeze had sprung up, rustling an evening paper on the table. It struck at Lucia with a touch of chill. She crossed the room and closed the terrace door. Schnucke stirred uneasily.

The Captain came back and stood quite still in the foyer while Schnucke trotted up to his side. "Bob Morse promised to help me, Lucia. Don't worry. I'll get in touch with you as soon as I find out anything more. Good night." He was gone before she could make a move to accompany him to the door.

Paul came back but didn't sit down. "He must have been rooting around in the dirt under the bushes. God knows what for. Are you going to stay here tonight?"

"No," said Lucia, "but I want to straighten out some things in my room."

"Shall I see you back to the hotel?"

"Don't be silly, Paul."

"Look," he said quickly, "I know things aren't so hot right now. If you don't want me to hang around drawing my salary, say so. I can get another job in five minutes today."

"You want to leave?" Lucia asked him.

He said, "Hell, no. If I can be of any help I'll stick around. But you might ask Larmar tomorrow. He might want to let me go. I think I'll turn in."

Lucia said, "Good night," and added, "That's thoughtful of you, Paul."

"Forget it, and keep your chin up." He went into his room and closed the door.

She sorted clothes for half an hour, packing another suitcase, then started going through her desk. Old bills and old letters, stirring up old memories. Bills that had been paid and letters that had been answered. Caught in a sudden wave of irritation, she began to tear them up and throw them away.

It was long past midnight when she finished.

The wind had strengthened and a sudden gust dashed rain through her open window. Lucia got up and closed it, still not quite conscious that a heavy summer storm had broken. A streak of lightning flashed downward to release a rumbling bomb of thunder.

Larmar had always comforted her during thunderstorms, but Larmar was in jail.

Life and thoughtlessness and carelessness had caught up with her. She was in a home that wasn't a home, an apartment that was a house for death by violence. Her home had become a hotel room, Lucia Jordan's hideaway. Now she was caught in limbo where lightning flashed and thunder rolled.

Fear of the storm became predominant. It was terrible to know that you had a room where you couldn't go and a home where you couldn't stay. Yet, the terrace, and the gun room, and the memories were worse than the raging storm.

She snapped the suitcase shut, set her teeth and put out the lights. For an instant she stopped in the study, moved by an impulse to awaken Paul. She dismissed it instantly and opened the front door.

The man with the deep cleft scar in his chin was standing outside in the hall.

Lucia drew back into the foyer, her throat muscles tied tight with panic.

"I want to talk to you, Mrs. Jordan." His hand went against the panel, pushing the door as he followed her in.

The door clicked shut, leaving them both in blackness, and still she couldn't call.

He was breathing close as she found the switch and lit the light in the hall.

"Who are you?" she managed to say, and each word hurt.

"You needn't be frightened." He stepped a little closer, backing her into the study. "I want to talk to you, that's all."

She found the lamp and lit it.

"Sit down," he said.

Lucia obeyed him for there was a glow in his eyes that was not quite human, as though they'd seen so many horrors that another could make no difference.

He took a chair quite near her and his coat stretched tight again across the width of his shoulders as it had in the hotel lobby.

Screaming seemed futile, for the unreality had descended once more. There was a storm off stage, with thunder and lightning and she was caught on the scene with every exit barred. Somewhere off stage there were other actors, but she had to find the

cue to bring them on. Then they might come again and play
their silly parts—Larmar and Bob and Duncan Maclain and Paul.

"Gallagher's the name," he said. "Did you ever hear it?"

"Never." Her head kept turning back and forth with the
motions of a panicked sparrow. "What do you want? I've never
heard of you."

"That's a hot one, isn't it?" His wide lips worked in a grimace.
"The name Martin Gallagher means nothing at all to your
murdering husband and you?"

"Nothing," said Lucia.

"You're a lying bitch!" His hands grew tighter on the arms of
the chair. "Your husband knew she was married. But she didn't
think her darling Martin would ever get back from the war."

Lucia could only say, "Who?"

"That little slut, Rose Gallagher. She was a slut all right, but I
loved her." He watched Lucia's face unblinkingly. "Maybe you
knew her better by her phony name of Troy." His heavy wide
shoulders hunched forward. "Maybe it's me that should be killing you."

". . . it will be now;"

I

Inspector Larry Davis' office at police headquarters on Centre Street was a simple affair. A broad flat desk dominated one corner. The decorations were a framed print of Franklin Delano Roosevelt and several uncomfortable wooden chairs ranged along the wall. On the other side of the office, a long oak table supported a few dusty copies of magazines pertinent to the police profession. The magazines signally failed to produce a touch of home.

In back of his desk, the inspector was busy leafing through the contents of a folder. Duncan Maclain occupied a chair at the end of the table. Bob Morse and Lucia were vainly trying to attain positions of ease in two of the chairs along the wall. Seated across the desk from Davis, Jess Ferguson, somehow managing to look more rumpled than ever, was applying his legal training to the task of reading the upside down contents of Davis' folder, a neat trick since his eyes were watching the progress of a blue bottle fly climbing the wall.

The fly took wing and zoomed across the office to light near Maclain. Schnucke snapped at it in passing and missed, then lay down again.

Davis shut up the folder and put it in a drawer. His gray eyes fixed on the lawyer, he said interestedly, "That's supposed to be a private file, Mr. Ferguson. Did you manage to read it all?"

"I got enough to satisfy me," Ferguson said quite unperturbed.

The inspector took a rubber band from a tray on his desk and stretched it out thin. "I had this fellow Gallagher picked up this morning, as you asked me to, Mr. Ferguson."

"What did you do with him?"

Davis snapped the rubber band with his strong white teeth making it sing. "Archer questioned him and we let him go. There was nothing we could hold him for."

"He threatened to kill me last night," Lucia put in.

Davis said, "I don't agree, Mrs. Jordan. Martin Gallagher's an ex-cop, and his record's not bad. He enlisted in the Army and was discharged after seeing a lot of fighting out in the Pacific."

Maclain pursed his lips and said, "He's a manly little fellow from what you tell me, Lucia. A bit slap-happy, that's all."

The inspector relaxed his rubber band and tucked it away tenderly beside the file in his drawer. "Don't try to needle me, Maclain. Gallagher got out of a hospital in San Francisco and came back here looking for his wife. He hadn't heard from her since he joined the Army."

"And some time previous to that," remarked Ferguson, staring at the ceiling, "from what I could read in the report in your file."

"Well, maybe he was that much more anxious to find her," said Davis. "Being an ex-cop, he started making inquiries. He managed to locate a couple of men who had known her."

"That must have been a brilliant piece of police work." Bob Morse treated himself to a hearty yawn.

The inspector said, "If the four of you think you're going to get any place by riding me, you're crazy."

"My God, you're touchy this morning, Larry," Maclain protested soothingly. "We're merely trying to find out why this pal of yours broke into Lucia's apartment last night."

"He's not a pal of mine and he didn't break in anywhere." Davis glared truculently around the office. "He found out that his wife had sung in a night club under the name of Troy. Then he saw what had happened in the papers. Well, how would any of you feel if you'd found out your wife had been shot? Do you think that it would fill your heart with joy?"

"I don't know," said Bob. "The two I've had quit me to collect alimony."

"Well, Gallagher got mad," Davis continued. "He wanted more information and decided he could get it from Mrs. Jordan, so he went up to her apartment to ask her some questions. She let him in, he asked his questions, and went away satisfied. So far as I can see, that's about all."

"Was it necessary," Maclain inquired gently, "for him to scare her half to death by trailing her from her hotel to the apartment, waiting till everyone had left and popping up like that in the hall?"

"Did you see him following you, Mrs. Jordan?" asked Davis.

"How else would an ex-policeman find her?" Bob wanted to know. "He'd never think of looking her up in the telephone directory. I remember one case I covered—"

"I don't want to hear about it," said Davis. "You let him in yourself, Mrs. Jordan. He claims he was just about to ring the bell when you stepped out of your door. He told you he just wanted to talk to you. After all, it seems quite natural to me. Your husband—"

"Did what?" asked Ferguson, still intent on the ceiling.

"That's for the courts to decide." The inspector shrugged.

"Well, I think this Gallagher's dangerous," said Ferguson, mussing his hair until he resembled an angry porcupine. "There's another part of that report that you haven't mentioned."

"It's confidential." The inspector's steel trap mouth set itself uncompromisingly.

Morse asked, "Are you referring to the fact that Gallagher was discharged from the Army as a mental case, Inspector?"

"Who told you that?" Davis looked suspiciously from Ferguson to the report in his partly open drawer.

"I've been doing a little digging myself since the Captain called me this morning." Bob Morse was smug. "I suppose it will be all right for me to mention in the paper that this loose nut's running around New York frightening defenseless women into spasms, but that the department's officially labeled him harmless."

"You could, but you won't," said Davis. "You and the *Globe-Tribune* know too much about the libel law."

Bob reached into his pocket and took out a few sheets of flimsy folded in three and covered with notes in his heavy black scrawl. "Troy was killed on Thursday afternoon." His round face wrinkled with study. "On Tuesday, two days before she was shot, a husband—" he paused and puffed out his cheeks, "Shall we say an insanely jealous husband?—arrived in New York looking for her."

"A husband quite familiar with firearms," put in Duncan Maclain. "A husband trained in their niceties and use in two proficient schools, the police force and the Army. Am I right, Bob?"

"You bet your life you're right," Morse agreed readily. "Hubby started digging up unsavory facts as soon as he hit here. Wifey may have changed her name from Rose Gallagher to something else but it wasn't difficult for this ex-policeman to smell out the trail of this girl called Troy. She had a lot of angles, that baby. You'll admit that, won't you, Inspector? I mean, I could use that safely without running foul of the libel law?"

Davis gave a noncommittal grunt and finally said, "The fact

that she was ripe for killing doesn't help Mr. Jordan any that I can see."

The Captain muttered, "Not at all, Larry, not at all. Go on, Bob, read us some more of his history. Take us right up to last night if you can, to the time he paid Lucia a call."

Bob looked up over the top of his notes with the anticipatory expression of an overstuffed Billikin. "There were others besides Larmar Jordan interested in Troy's night club project, Inspector. Ex-patrolman Gallagher discovered that his dizzy darling had been dining in public with a certain respected citizen by the name of—" he paused and consulted his notes, "Daniel Pine."

Jess Ferguson chuckled way down in his throat and said, "Unh-oh!"

The inspector appeared not to have heard. He searched his pockets carefully and finally took a toothpick from a box in his lower left hand desk drawer.

"Of course," said Bob, "the world is full of Pines and lots of them must be named Daniel."

Davis gripped the toothpick firmly and went to work on the upper row.

"This one lives out in Plandome, Long Island," said Morse with the expression of an angel. "Maybe he's the same guy whose airplane factory was awarded the Navy 'E'. I wouldn't know."

"No, you wouldn't know," the inspector intoned viciously. Pulling himself up close to his desk he began to push papers to one side, giving himself more room. Planting both elbows in the cleared away space, he put his chin on his clenched up fists. Under his gray mustache the toothpick projected menacingly. "Now listen, I'm a friendly sort of a guy, Maclain, and I have a high respect for your ability."

The Captain grinned. "You also have a habit of petting me before you pot me, Larry. What's the matter? Did Daniel Pine get under your skin?"

"You're damn right he did!" Davis spat the toothpick in a waste basket three feet away. "A murder's a murder to the Homicide Squad and I feel sorry as the next one for innocent people who get hurt. Furthermore, I don't blame you and Mrs. Jordan for making every effort you can to save her husband. But there're limits, by God, there're limits." His usually calm voice crept up half an octave. "So the Singleton girl had dinner with Daniel Pine? So she had dinner with him. So what? Morse hasn't discovered anything that the department doesn't know."

"He's discovered something that the department has kept almighty quiet," said Duncan Maclain.

"You're damn tootin' we've kept it quiet. Dan Pine's an important figure. He's manufacturing aircraft for our lads overseas and we need all the aircraft we can get if we're going to win."

The Captain began to whistle *The Stars and Stripes Forever,* and Schnucke looked up inquiringly.

Davis said, "Go ahead and clown your head off. Pine's a widower and he has a right to have dinner with anybody he wants to. What the hell do you hope to gain by ringing him in?"

Bob said, "Tut-tut, Inspector. Your wronged ex-policeman went out to Plandome to talk with him."

"That girl must have had a bicycle," Ferguson remarked to the ceiling and added softly, "No, no, those tycoons who manufacture airplanes have plenty of gasoline. He could have driven her out and in."

Davis slapped his hand down hard on the desk in a sudden flash of anger. "You can't break my case against Jordan,

Ferguson, neither you nor Maclain. Pulling a piece of political codfish up and down under my nostrils isn't going to help you win. I'm asking you one more time what the hell's the idea of turning up stones and producing Dan Pine? Where does he fit in?"

"If I can prove he had just as much motive for killing Troy as Larmar had, it should make an awfully good story for Bob's paper," said Duncan Maclain.

"Well, try to prove he was there when the girl was shot," said Davis, calm again.

"Now that's an idea, Larry." The Captain reached down and stroked Schnucke's back. "Dan Pine and your sailor."

"What sailor?" asked Davis.

"Oh, don't you know your boy friend Gallagher with the gentle disposition also spent three years in the Merchant Marine?"

"Climbing masts," said Morse, clucking his tongue.

The Captain nodded agreement and stood up to turn his back on Davis and face the window. "I've a lot of ideas about this perfect case of yours, Larry. Maybe I'll prove that this ex-sailor climbed up six stories from the terrace below and plugged the girl."

"Try it," said Davis.

The Captain gently fingered the lobe of one ear. "Maybe I will at that, Larry. Maybe it will give me a brand-new place to begin."

2

The Captain caught a cab from Centre Street up to the Pennsylvania station, and made the ride with his mind divided between totting up the fare and contemplating some of the past history of Daniel Pine.

Many people had underrated Duncan Maclain, forgetting that

interest in current events and assimilation of knowledge are meat and drink to the blind. The Captain's relaxations were those of any normal man of more than average wealth, and controlling, in addition, a profitable business.

He played a masterly game of contract bridge and enjoyed it to the limit, although he always refused to deal for himself, pointing out with a smile that Braille marked cards which couldn't be seen by his partner or his opponents were easily readable in dealing when the dealer was blind.

His game of chess was withering to most amateurs. With the same precision which enabled him to visualize and retain the moves on a setup chess board, he kept a dossier of the lives of current public figures filed away in the archives of his capacious mind. A few salient facts obtained that morning from Bob Morse had added to his knowledge of Daniel Pine.

Pine was a fighter. Born of an humble family, and without much education, he had started work early in the automobile plants in Detroit, to be lost in that beehive for several years and to emerge as a full-fledged engineer. From that point on by sheer hard work and jerking on his boot-straps, he had pulled himself far up the assembly line.

The war had boosted him into real prominence. Derisive of red tape and scornful of senatorial interference, he had jammed through a profit-sharing system for his employees. The men and women working for him had liked it so well that the Daniel Pine Associates had topped every aircraft factory in the country for planes produced during the year. The Captain decided that the very qualities that had made Daniel Pine successful might also make him a man to fear.

The cab rolled down the Long Island ramp at the station.

Maclain said, "Thank you," and handed the driver his fare plus a quarter tip. "The two bits," he said with a grin, "are because you made good time but didn't shake my liver out getting me here."

"Are you blind, mister?" the driver asked, throwing up his flag.

"Very," said Maclain.

"Maybe the dog talks." The driver leaned over to take a look at Schnucke.

"Your meter talks," said Duncan Maclain. "It makes a click for every nickel. You can add that to twenty cents when you put down your flag. Listen to it yourself sometime when you have nothing else to do. It should be music in your ears."

"Nuts," said the driver as Maclain strode off, following Schnucke. "Six more months of hacking in this burg and I'll be goin' queer."

It seemed strange that life could offer compensations for blindness, yet the Captain had found many; escape from bores by departing abruptly as though he hadn't noticed that anyone was near; utter relaxation in music and talking books; the ability to read himself to sleep on long cold nights with a volume in Braille tucked under the covers beside him and the quilt pulled up to his chin.

There was another compensation in the Long Island station. Packed full with a Saturday crowd, others might be jostled and pushed and wait in line for hours. The Captain had found that wherever he went, Schnucke was a passport that always let him in.

Yet, there was sadness too, for people were only voices to Duncan Maclain and his ears heard much that others missed. A station was a place of parting and Duncan Maclain, listening to whispers, could sense the giant heartache under America's grin.

A hand reached out and took his arm. A voice said, "Where're you going, Captain?"

The voice clicked into place as a man with eyes will recognize a friend.

"Plandome, Donovan. With this mob here, you fellows on the pickpocket squad must be taking it on the chin."

"Darn my hide! I've listened to Davis and Archer talk about you for years, Captain, and I've known you—for how many now?"

"Seven," said Maclain.

"And still I don't believe it," said Donovan forcefully. "My own cousin from California spoke to me here last week and me who can pick out five hundred dips by sight didn't know him. Yet, a word to you and you have me labeled."

The Captain laughed. "Try shutting your eyes and keeping them closed for twenty years, Donovan. Then come up to see me and I'll teach you to pick out people by sound."

"Yeah," said Donovan, "I'll let you know when I want to begin." He led the Captain to the window and bought his round trip ticket. As he returned the change, he asked Maclain, "How do you know if that bill you gave me is a one or a five or a ten?"

"Cappo, my valet, folds them for me," said Duncan Maclain. "They're in different shapes. Then I ask the cashier to tell me what bills I'm getting and fold them myself if I get change for a ten. Simple, isn't it?"

"The way you tell it," said Donovan. "I'll take you down to your train. They've a lot of new gatemen on duty and they may not want to let Schnucke in."

"You might locate me in the smoker," said Maclain. "And don't seat me by any of your pickpocket friends."

"Most of them are in the Army." The detective smiled. "I know half a dozen that will give the Gestapo a headache if they ever land in Berlin. Happy landings!" He seated Maclain and was gone.

The Captain sat with his eyes closed tight as the overladen train jerked its way out onto Long Island. He wasn't asleep. He had analyzed a set of facts which had been collated by the efficient police and dumped into his lap labeled murder. He was frankly troubled because the results of his analysis were still quite hazy.

His trip to Plandome was an impulse. Dan Pine might be out or in. He hadn't stopped to inquire. Even if he was home, the Captain's chances of seeing him without an appointment were slim. Maclain didn't particularly care.

Larmar Jordan's motives for killing Troy didn't suit him. Larmar was the creative type, and the murder of Troy was a hardheaded piece of business. The Captain wanted to find a reagent to clarify things.

Dan Pine had a head as hard as the statue of Rodin's Thinker. Given a motive, Pine would be far more likely than Larmar Jordan to dust off a pestiferous female with a Buchel pistol. The best way to find out if Troy had really been pestiferous was by talking to Daniel Pine.

Even if he didn't get to see him, the trip out and back was relaxing and gave one time to think. Whatever happened, a check on Pine's relationship with Troy could do no harm, and at least it offered the solace of a concrete place to begin.

Yet, at the end of the ride, the Captain found he was tired and hot. When a voice at the station said, "Taxi, mister?" the Captain was glad to give Pine's address and lean back on the worn cushions.

The driver moved off with a barrage of gears and drove half a mile in silence.

Finally he asked, "Been out here before?"

"No," said Maclain.

"Know Mr. Pine?"

"No." Maclain heard the driver twist in his seat and turn to watch the road again.

"I've been trying to get a job in his plant. He's got a waiting list of thirty thousand. I suppose you've got an appointment to see him."

"I'm blind," said Duncan Maclain.

"I mean to say, I suppose you've got an appointment to talk with him."

"No," the Captain said again.

The driver was worried. "You shouldn't have come all the way out here without an appointment. He's got a gatehouse at the entrance to his grounds. Unless you've got an appointment, they won't let me drive in."

"Did you ever hear of the Maharaja of Landripur?" asked Maclain.

"No sir, I never did." The driver slowed down the car.

"Then I can speak freely," said Duncan Maclain. "I got into his harem without an appointment."

"Well, he ain't Daniel Pine," said the driver, speeding up again, "and there's the gatehouse, and there's your chance to do your stuff, brother."

The car turned right. Maclain heard the wheels crunch on gravel and sounds of footsteps on a short asphalt walk.

Someone stopped by the car and stuck his head inside. "I'm Dan Pine," a voice said heartily. "I've been waiting for you, Captain Maclain."

3

Seated on the terrace in back of Pine's house with a fragrant mint julep beside him, Duncan Maclain listened to the splash and laughter of half a dozen guests reveling in the swimming pool a short distance away. From across the glass-topped table beside him, the Captain caught an occasional whiff of Dan Pine's private smoking mixture. In a matter of fifteen minutes, he had developed a growing respect for the qualities of his host.

Pine was wearing a flannel shirt, slacks, and rubber-soled shoes. That much Maclain had determined from his short walk beside him. He was wearing something else which interested the Captain much more—a cloak of boyish geniality which covered the real man as a brightly striped bathrobe might envelop a strong bronzed body.

Somewhere Maclain had heard him described as a modern Caesar. From that bit of hearsay, the Captain pictured Pine, not inaccurately, as endowed with a Roman nose, straight brows over oval eyes, and a wide mouth dominating a chin which was deceptive because it didn't look too strong. Pine had already inadvertently told Maclain that his hair was thick and curly through a habit of occasionally smoothing it down with one hand. Hands on hair made sound.

Whatever the result might be, Maclain felt certain that he wouldn't be bored by pitting his wits against Dan Pine. The manufacturer was one of the few men he had met who didn't underrate him because he was blind.

"You haven't asked me how I knew you were coming," said Pine.

"Do I need to?" The Captain buried his nose in the fragrant mint and put down the heavy crystal glass with a sigh of satisfaction. "It's as obvious as the fact that you have a colored butler to make your mint juleps. You were having me followed and your man telephoned up from the station."

"I'm glad you told me. I'll fire him," said Pine.

"I wouldn't." The Captain's lips twisted with humor. "You'll never get a better one. I hadn't an idea in the world I was being trailed, and I'm a very tough subject. A persistent set of footsteps echoing around in back of me makes me nervous."

"Oh, so I'm the dope," said Pine. "I tipped you off myself by my greeting at the gate." He laughed, making very little noise but adding a perceptible trembling to the table.

"I don't believe in mind reading," said Duncan Maclain. "I didn't know I was coming out here myself until an hour before train time."

"Indeed? And what decided you then?"

"Your name came up at police headquarters, Mr. Pine."

"Hell, it's been up in Congress, and that hasn't worried me. What makes you think I'd get the jitters over a lot of dumb cops talking about Daniel Pine?"

Pipe smoke struck Maclain.

"That's what I came out here to find out." The Captain coughed gently. "Men with your money don't hire detectives to trail detectives unless they have the jitters, Mr. Pine. Getting mixed up with private operators not only indicates worry, but it takes a lot of time."

"Let's go inside," said Pine. He got up and took the Captain's arm.

They ascended the broad green bank with the grass soft under the Captain's feet, took two stone steps and crossed a stone porch to enter wide french doors. Grass matting marked a sunparlor; polished wood with scattered orientals signposted a hall.

Schnucke stayed close to the Captain's right side, sulking at Pine's usurping her place on the left.

They crossed a sill.

Pine said, "Sit down," and closed a door.

"A nice place you have," Maclain remarked conversationally. The sound of his own voice measured the room; fifteen to twenty feet wide; twenty-five or thirty feet long; ceiling high; cabinets along each wall.

"I paid a lot for it," said Pine.

The Captain repressed an inclination to tell him the anecdote about Moss Hart and Wolcott Gibbs in which Hart had told Gibbs it had cost him a hundred thousand dollars to move a certain elm tree from the top of a hill to his lawn, and Gibbs had said it showed what God could do if he had money.

Everything was friendly, but it was the friendliness of a handshake in the prize ring after the gloves are on.

"You're a busy man yourself, Captain Maclain. I read of your work in Hartford when you ran down that spy ring. You're cleverer than most people think."

"I paid a lot for it," said Maclain.

Pine gave his silent laugh. "You're not going to tell me anything, are you? Well, go ahead and be delightfully insulting. Maybe it will egg me on."

"We can trade," said Maclain. "I want to know why you were having me followed, and you want to know why I came."

"Very well, we'll lie quite frankly."

"I have nothing to lie about," said Maclain.

"Okay, we won't lie." Pine got up and started a slow mechanical pacing. "I'm a widower. I like women, and I have a lot of money. I expect to be gouged, reasonably of course, but that puts me in the position of knowing what they want before I make their acquaintance. Then, the chiselers have to be smart and attractive. Taking it all together, it saves a lot of time."

"It creates a certain amount of excitement," the Captain offered.

"And headaches," added Pine. "I met a girl a few months ago that looked expensive but interesting. She turned out to be both."

"If her name was Singleton, you're not the only one she's hooked," said Duncan Maclain.

"For a blind man, you keep your eyes damn wide open," remarked Pine. He stopped in front of the Captain's chair. "Her name was Singleton all right, but as a matter of fact, she didn't get expensive until she got herself murdered. Prior to that, she hadn't hooked me for a dime, barring a few dinners, of course, which are always part of the game."

The Captain took out his silver lighter and twisted it between his fingers. "So you didn't get worried then until after she was killed."

"I never get worried," said Pine. "I protect myself. Every newshawk in the country has an eye on Daniel Pine. The Singleton girl had a husband." He took a pair of horn-rimmed glasses from the pocket of his flannel shirt, put them on and looked closer at Maclain. "Did you know that?"

"I heard of him this morning," the Captain admitted.

"I heard of him night before last," said Pine. "He came out to the plant to see me."

"Wanting money?"

"I'd have had him arrested if he wanted money," said Pine and started walking again. "Apparently, all he wanted was information about what his wife had been doing while he was away. I didn't have any to give him, but I had him followed."

"And me." The Captain chuckled.

"Well, I sort of included you on the list when I heard that

Mrs. Jordan had called you in to attempt to clear her husband."

"I didn't know that was public property."

"Money can buy you lots of things before the newspapers get them," said Pine.

"Including headaches."

"Yes," agreed Pine. "It's the job of this detective agency I have to act as aspirin."

He stopped his walking and began to crack his knuckles. "I could tell you quite a bit about Troy Singleton if I wanted to. I had her followed for some time. Since she was killed, I've had a lot of other people followed, people who might be interested in trying to build up something that didn't exist between Singleton and Pine."

"And you intend to continue having them followed?"

"Until Jordan's safe in the chair," said Pine.

The Captain got up, and holding onto Schnucke's U-shaped brace, started a tour of the room. He walked to one end, brushing the walls two or three times with his finger tips, then crossed and came back on the other side, making a circle around Pine. Back at his chair, he sat down.

The manufacturer narrowed his eyes and turned his head slowly to trace the Captain's tour.

"Well, what do you make of it?" he asked Maclain.

"You must have twice as many guns as Jordan," the Captain told him.

"Who told you I had guns?" asked Pine.

"I read your profile," said Maclain. "I have means of reading even if I am blind."

"Are you interested in guns?"

"Very." The Captain placed the tips of his long fingers together and made a tent on one knee. "Did you ever hear of a Harpers

Ferry flintlock pistol dated eighteen hundred and four, Mr. Pine?"

"Just one, and I have it," said Pine.

"That's most interesting. I'd like to examine it some time."

"You can examine it now," said Pine.

Keys rattled and Maclain heard the sound of a sliding glass door. He waited an instant, then broke the tent on his knee and stretched out one hand.

Pine watched with interest as the Captain's educated fingers slowly promenaded along every contour of the flintlock gun.

"An interesting piece," said Duncan Maclain. "I examined one just like it last night." He returned the pistol.

"If it was a Harpers Ferry flintlock dated eighteen hundred and four, it was a fake," said Pine.

"That's right," Maclain agreed. "The date on it had been filed off and changed. But Larmar Jordan thinks it's genuine. Where did you get yours?"

"That's my business, Captain," said Pine.

4

If Duncan Maclain clung to any fetish while traveling through his years of darkness, it was that of being careful. He liked to point out that a blind man who learned to type must master one cardinal rule—the rule of no mistakes. A blind typist who struck a wrong letter must start all over again for his attempts to erase were clumsy and pitiful things.

Moving too fast and without his usual calm consideration had at one time trapped the Captain and Spud in a burning building, and very nearly ended their career. From that time onward, Maclain had approached every undertaking on the assumption that death was very near.

The circumstances connected with Troy Singleton were different. Perhaps it was the people involved, Larmar and Lucia, Paul Hirst and Bob Morse, Brownie, and Sarah Hanley. They were ordinary New Yorkers to Duncan Maclain, friends of the woman he loved, who had unfortunately gotten themselves into a nasty jam.

Gallagher, of course, might be dangerous due to his mental condition. Dan Pine was saber-toothed but he worked within the law, using a battery of large caliber lawyers.

The fact that Troy Singleton was dead should have been a stop light to Duncan Maclain. He had heard the saying that blood begets blood and murder is the child of murder. Yet, for once in his life, he became so concentrated on the fascinating technical possibilities of a killing that the human element fell into shadow. It was doubly dangerous. It lowered his guard and allowed him to act without full premeditation.

Yet, it wasn't exactly carelessness. There had been a lulling quality and leisureliness of pace surrounding every step of his efforts to put Larmar Jordan in the clear.

It was past six when Cappo admitted him to the penthouse far above Seventy-second Street and Riverside Drive, and said with a touch of reproach, "You're late, Captain. The ladies is already here."

"The ladies?" Maclain turned his hat and Schnucke over to his butler-valet.

"Miss Sybella and Mrs. Jordan. I mixed them cocktails."

"That's fine." Maclain was in a good humor warmed with a pleasant elation over the outcome of his visit to Pine.

He went into the office stretching out both hands.

"Well, this is delightful."

"Yes, isn't it, darling?" Sybella said amused. "You asked me to invite Lucia to dinner with us tonight." She took his hand and glanced at her tiny wrist watch. "I think five o'clock was the time set for you to meet us here."

"I've been out on Long Island." Maclain disengaged her fingers with an affectionate pat, and went to sit back of his desk. It was home to him—a refuge where he knew the exact location of every object.

Sybella brought him a cocktail and placed it in the metal tray affixed to his desk where he could find it without groping.

He sipped his drink and said contritely, "I'm sorry to be late, Lucia, but I'm working hard."

"With any results?"

"There's a lot more to be done before I can tell." He returned his drink to the metal tray, and pushed a button behind him.

Lucia started as a voice came through a loud speaker set in the wall. "When you hear the signal, it will be exactly six-eighteen."

Sybella said, "You should warn people about that, Duncan. I jumped a foot the first time I heard it and this is Lucia's first visit here."

"My life is full of gadgets," said Duncan Maclain, and asked, "Where's Rena?".

"She left for Washington this afternoon to spend a few days with Spud," Sybella explained.

He leaned back in his chair, his rugged face mapped deep with lines of concentration. Sybella, who had a second sight about his moods, stayed silent, but Lucia asked,

"Is something the matter, Captain?"

He finished his cocktail but didn't answer. After a while he said half aloud, "I wish to God that Spud was here."

"It has been a long time since he went to Washington, hasn't it?" Sybella was speaking more to herself than to the Captain. "It's over a year."

She refrained from saying the Captain's abrupt proposal of marriage over the telephone had also been made more than a year before.

But sensitive to every cadence of Sybella's remarks, he picked up the thought from her tone. "I don't know how I would have carried on without your company, darling. You've been a dear."

"Yes," she said, making an honest attempt not to hurt him with irony. "At least both of us understand that while we enjoy each other's company, we are always free to spend some evenings alone."

Either he hadn't heard her or he was immersed in his problem again. Sybella decided it was the latter, for he drew himself up close to the desk and took the inevitable fifty-piece jigsaw puzzle from the right-hand drawer, dumping the pieces into a pile before him.

Lucia watched stolidly with the air of an unwilling believer held in spite of herself by a voodoo priestess shaking a hypnotizing charm.

The Captain's jigsaw puzzle was a fount of ideas which seldom failed him. By following the curves and angles of the pieces with the tips of his fingers, he had learned through years of practice to put the puzzle together faster than a man who could see.

Yet, when he was puzzled himself, when his thoughts were confused, the picture at his finger tips was slow to take form. He sat there now, seemingly loath to begin, gently prodding the tiny pile with his index finger, then stirring it out into smoothness with a circular motion of his arm.

Sybella lit a cigarette. The scratch of the match brought the Captain's head around, to hold her for a second with the blankness of his stare.

"There are things connected with Troy Singleton's murder," he said at last, "that even a blind man can't see. What would your husband have gained, Lucia, by killing that girl?"

"Nothing," she whispered.

Again the Captain wasn't listening. "She had his money, plunged into a foolish venture. Davis claimed she wanted to marry him. I don't think that's true." Maclain turned from Sybella and raised his eyebrows. "She departed from the cocktail party without any trouble on Wednesday afternoon. I think she would have walked out of Larmar's existence just as readily."

The Captain's fingers had found two pieces of the puzzle. He picked them up, one in each hand and joined them daintily; then laying them flat on the desk, he pressed them down with his thumb, and began to talk again.

"It's hard to believe in logic, Lucia, and then explain away a man alone in his apartment, a dead girl, and a bullet in her which fits that man's own gun."

"He didn't do it," said Lucia.

"Then we have to dismiss our logic," said Duncan Maclain. "We have to start out on a fresh new trail. If Larmar didn't kill her, I have to write a fairy story and present it to Davis and Archer. I have to make it so interesting and so convincing that two of the slickest, hardest-headed cops in Gotham will swallow it and turn around to help me."

His mobile lips set tight until he found another piece which built the start of his puzzle to three. His head shook slowly in a motion that might have been despair.

"And by God, ladies, that's going to be some fun! Duncan Maclain against the department of ballistics. Duncan Maclain, blind as a bat and batty as a loon, trying to tell a man like Davis that some mechanical means was used to fire that Buchel gun."

Sybella leaned forward, her hands clasped tightly. "What are you driving at, Duncan?"

"Just what I said," he told her with irritation. "The Buchel pistol killed her. If Larmar didn't pull the trigger, what did?"

"The carillon." Lucia discovered that she had twisted her handkerchief into a ball. "Is that what you meant last night when you said that the man in the tower across the street might have shot her? The man who plays the carillon?"

"The science of crime progresses," said Duncan Maclain. "A year ago I met a man who discovered a means of pushing people out of windows when he wasn't there. For a time, I even agreed with Davis and Archer when they said it couldn't be done. To-day I don't know. If I manage to save your husband, Lucia, it will be on account of the crime I solved last year. It reduced me to a state of doubt where I even believe that a carillon can be used to fire a gun. That's why I wish that Spud was here."

"Why do you need Spud?" asked Sybella.

"Because I need more dope on the Singleton girl," said Duncan Maclain. "There will be traces in her apartment he would find. I want to know whom she loved, and whom she lived with, and what she kept, and what she wore, and what she threw away. If I'm going to save Larmar, I've got to know things about that girl that nobody will ever tell me."

"I'll go myself," said Lucia. "I'll get in."

"You and your parade," said Duncan Maclain. "You may not know it, Lucia, but you and I and Paul and everybody within a radius of ten blocks of the Arday Apartments are like kites. Not only the police department, but a detective agency employed by Daniel Pine has operators on our trail."

"There must be some way, Captain." Lucia was close to hysteria. "I can't wait very much longer to get Larmar out of jail."

"It's the best place for him," said Duncan Maclain. "If I'm right, Troy sat herself down in front of a bullet intended for your husband. You'd better leave him where he is. The next time this killer tries to get your husband, he may not fail."

Sybella stood up and said softly, "There's nobody on my trail. Let's go and eat dinner, darling. Then I have to run along."

The Captain didn't hear her. Occupying his mind again were words of Bob Morse's picked out of *Hamlet*.

"'Sdeath! Captain Maclain—if it be not to come, it will be now!"

". . . if it be not now,"

I

THE CAPTAIN took them to the Waldorf.

When Sybella excused herself after dinner, leaving him and Lucia, she had no thought of any histrionic adventure. Obtaining admission to a murdered girl's apartment was a simple business proposition to be carried out with dispatch like any other business deal. A friend was in trouble. Sybella was sure and resourceful. It might be an intriguing problem but it certainly couldn't be difficult to obtain the information wanted by Duncan Maclain.

Through smartness and ingenuity, Sybella had built herself a profitable business which she operated under the name of the Richelieu Novelty and Decorating Company. Her apartment above the modern streamlined shop at Fifty-fourth and Madison had proved a haven for Duncan Maclain. She enjoyed watching him drink in the beauty of her carefully selected possessions through his fingertips. She found it restful to contemplate his utter relaxation against the smooth silk fabric of her favorite chair.

But it was the man who fascinated her, and not his business. Somehow, although she had been very close to him for over a year, his profession seemed remote and distorted. It was exciting to hear his calm narration of close escapes, but his unconscious habit of understatement robbed his adventures of personal reality, and placed them in the category of fiction.

Sybella's thrills were vicarious. She had never considered for a moment that personal danger might accrue from close association with Captain Duncan Maclain. If such an element had been present in Sybella's make-up, if she had possessed the slightest touch of concern for her own safety or Maclain's, the Captain might have sensed it too, and been on guard.

It was her overwhelming confidence in him which made him love her. It was unfortunate that it also made her a trifle fool-hardy. There was a job to be done. Sybella believed in approaching jobs by the shortest possible route.

Sybella had a taxi in mind until she remembered that taxi rides were easily traced. This promised to be fun. She took a casual look around the crowded lobby but was unable to single out any individuals mysterious enough to be following Lucia and Mac-lain.

She left the hotel on the Lexington Avenue side and walked unhurriedly to the subway station at Fifty-first Street. It was very doubtful that the police or Daniel Pine would be interested in Sybella Ford; she was too remote from the Jordan family. Nevertheless she took a few precautions to assure herself that she was not being followed.

"I want to know whom she loved, and whom she lived with; what she kept, and what she wore, and what she threw away." The Captain's words came back to her in monotonous rhythm, blending into the racket of the short ride on the subway train.

By the time she got off at Seventy-seventh Street, she had worked out a scheme. It involved a little lying but not much risk. It was true the police could trace her visit afterward—that didn't worry her. She had plenty of faith in the Captain's ability to take care of any unpleasantness which might arise through her search of Troy's effects.

The immediate problem was getting in. She worked out further details on her walk up Lexington to Eighty-first. She counted on her appearance and plausibility, with a few dollars added, to put over a story with the janitor.

It might work if she gave him a business card and said that Troy Singleton had bought furniture from the Richelieu Company which had never been paid for and that she, Sybella, wanted to take an inventory. Putting herself in the janitor's place, she decided that wasn't good enough. Why would a decorator show up after nine on Saturday night to inventory furniture? The janitor would be sure to stick around anyhow if he let her in.

She stopped and stared into a darkened shop window near Eighty-first Street, searching for a new line of attack and wishing she had had some comprehensive training in picking locks.

She decided to be Troy's sister. That seemed better. She'd just arrived in New York from Washington and her baggage was still at the station. Washington was always impressive. She had to be back by Monday. In the meantime, it was necessary that she get her dear dead sister's effects together. The furniture might fail; sympathy for a sad-eyed sister, plus ten dollars, might win.

Satisfied, she turned east on Eighty-first Street and stopped around the corner, seized by a tingling sense of criminality which was not entirely pleasant—criminals always stopped when they went around corners to make sure there was nobody on their trail.

A market on the corner was closed, but a light still showed inside. Sybella spent a moment studying beans, then walked the length of the block to Third Avenue where she turned and walked back. The street was deserted and very dim. A humid breeze trickled westward from the East River, carrying with it a harbor smell and the sound of deep-throated whistles.

She crossed to the uptown side and walked back to Lexington

Avenue again, studying Troy's former residence from across the street. It was a three-story brownstone house near the center of the block. The entrance was on the street level, but set back in a small square court, guarded by a high fence of pointed iron rails. Close to it were what appeared to be two private garages with the owners' homes above. They were closed now, and dark.

Sybella decided that Troy's house contained three apartments, one to a floor. The second and third stories were dark but a light in the ground floor window indicated that someone was in.

Two girls came out of a big apartment house near by and passed her with a babble of conversation. She waited until they had turned north on Lexington before she crossed the street again and walked through the iron-railed court. The sounds of a radio came through the lighted window.

Apparently the house contained five apartments instead of three, for five bell buttons set in brightly polished brass were inside the tiny lobby. Close by the buttons, a house phone hung on a hook. To the right of the phone another button was labeled Superintendent. Sybella pushed it, picked up the phone and waited hopefully. There was no answer and after a few seconds, she rang again.

In the back of the lobby a door opened, letting out light. An elderly woman came through the small lobby on her way to the street and smiled sympathetically at Sybella. Out in the court, the woman turned and came back in again.

"Were you looking for someone?"

"The janitor," Sybella explained.

The woman shook her head. "This is Saturday night. He's never in. Can I help you?"

"I'm trying to find an apartment."

The woman said, "There are none vacant in this house, I'm sure, unless—no, I'm sure there are none vacant in here. It's difficult to find anything in New York today. My son and his wife have been looking for some time and I finally had to take them in. Have you tried the big apartment house on the corner?"

"It has a sign up 'Fully rented'," Sybella told her.

"Oh, yes, I remember now." They walked out to the street together. The woman said, "Are you going toward Lexington?"

"No, I think I'll walk farther east." Sybella nodded and walked away.

When the helpful lady vanished, she returned to the house. This time she stopped on the street before she went in. How long would the police keep guard on the murdered girl's apartment? Was it a week or a day? She argued it out in her own mind and decided that so far as Troy was concerned, the police would have nothing to gain. They'd convinced themselves that Larmar was guilty. The chances were that they had searched Troy's apartment, obtained all the information they wanted, and then promptly gone away.

She went inside and confidently walked upstairs. Still, it was a relief to find no blue-clad figure sitting stolidly underneath the card on Troy Singleton's door. Of course, he might be inside, but he'd scarcely be sitting in the dark, and no light had showed from the street.

Sybella bent down and peered at the crack with her head close to the floor. The apartment was unquestionably dark.

She straightened up and gently tried the knob. The door was locked. Possessed by a streak of obstinacy, she walked to the rear of the hall where an unmarked door, probably service, proved to be locked as tightly as the front one.

A window in the back of the hall was open. Sybella looked out and saw the spiral outlines of a fire escape but it was too far away.

She pulled back in and tried another door which disclosed a stair well opening into the hall. It opened readily, but the stair well was black and uninviting. Two buckets of sand, a pump, a spade and some other fire equipment stood at one side on the bottom stair. Sybella struck a match, skirted the buckets and went on up.

At the top of the stairs, she unlocked a bolted door which opened onto a small roof garden. She went to the back and looked down over a low tile wall. A ladder leading down to the top of the fire escape was firmly fastened there. Sybella climbed over and down with no worse consequences than blackened hands and the ruination of an expensive dress by a six-inch tear.

The window opening onto the fire escape was fully raised. Inside a white net curtain hung down, moved limply by sporadic breaths of air.

She struck another match and by its light stepped through the window onto a kitchen chair.

2

In the corner an electric icebox clicked loudly and went to work with a steady hum.

The match burned out.

Sybella closed the window and pulled down the shade, then found a light switch by a door to the hall and flipped it up. A few seconds passed. Just as she had reached the conclusion that the lights were disconnected, vapor tubes over the sink and stove flickered pinkly and came on.

The kitchen was small, but neat and clean and showed evidence of competent handling. A maid, Sybella decided, or a cleaning woman, who had been there recently and carelessly left a window open so the place might air.

The kitchen cupboard with glass doors housed a set of china fine enough to catch Sybella's eye. Limoges dinner plates, gold encrusted and ostentatious, stood on a pile beside delicate plates and paper-thin cups and saucers.

Another part of the cupboard held six quarts of Lanson '28 champagne in wooden boxes. Obviously Troy Singleton hadn't stinted when she wanted to entertain.

The kitchen opened onto a fair-sized pantry with a built-in dining nook done in yellow. There was a sterling silver service in a mahogany case and several sets of fine handworked linen in a drawer.

Sybella put out the kitchen lights and turned on the lamp in the hall. The apartment was larger than she had thought, for the hall stretched nearly the full length of the building, with the pantry and kitchen at one end, and three doors opening off of it to the left. To her right were two more doors, one far to the front, and the other close at hand. She opened it a crack and looked out, discovering it was the service door she had tried outside.

The first door to the left led into a bedroom which might have come out of Sloane's window. Sybella found the shades were drawn and turned on twin lamps on the dressing table. Light struck back from the triple mirrors touching a wide footless bed of baby blue, with a quilted headboard of shimmering satin. A matching chaise longue stood in one corner. There was a bench in front of the dressing table. In front of one of the windows was a small puff chair.

The door to a commodious closet stood partly open. Sybella

pulled it wider and turned the closet light on. There were hat boxes on the shelves bearing labels of John-Frederics and Lilly Daché, and still more hats perched rakishly on big spring holders with rounded ends. An assorted collection of expensive shoes and slippers on slanting racks stood in an orderly row. The remainder of the closet was crowded with a fortune in frocks and coats, and suits and gowns.

Sybella thought rather grimly that living, Troy might have been a refutation anent the hackneyed statement concerning profit and crime. But Troy's warm rounded body had moved from the soft blue bed to a harder and colder sleeping place downtown. It wasn't the old saw that was dead. It was Troy.

"—what she kept and what she wore—"

Sybella shivered a little and started leafing through the clothes racks, gown by gown.

"—and whom she lived with—"

On the tenth hanger, under a chic fall suit that was older than the rest, she found a tie. It bore the tag of a Fifth Avenue men's shop that was notoriously expensive. It was blue and rich and thick and had been worn a lot. Sybella gave it a single glance and decided it didn't belong to Troy. Everything Troy owned was superlatively feminine. So far, the only incongruous note in the whole delightful apartment was the tie. Of course Troy had a husband, but from what Sybella had heard of Martin Gallagher, he'd be most unlikely to invest six or seven dollars in a handmade silk cravat.

She pulled it down and tucked it into her handbag, then finished her search of the closet. The only thing of interest was the tie.

She abandoned the closet and went through a drawer in the richly appointed dressing table. There was nothing there except an assortment of the small odds and ends possessed by any meticulous girl.

The bureau proved barren also, revealing nothing but handkerchiefs, stockings, and an array of dainty silk underwear in a sachet-scented drawer.

A door with a full length mirror led to the bathroom which had another door opening into the hall. Fresh initialed towels hung on the racks. A red rubber bathing cap made a spot of color against the white tile walls. The medicine cabinet held bath salts and powder, a safety razor with blades, and a box of nembutal.

Sybella examined the razor and saw that the blade it contained was rusty. Men were finicky about razor blades. She decided it belonged to Troy.

She put out all the lights and feeling much like Bluebeard's wife, walked to the remaining door near the front of the hall. It led into a sitting room. A light on Eighty-first Street threw each piece of furniture into dim relief. It showed up a curtained archway leading into an alcove across the room. A set of brass fireplace accouterments gleamed dully in front of the old-fashioned white marble mantel.

Sybella found that her nervousness had disappeared to be replaced by an almost arrogant self-confidence in her search of this dead girl's home.

She drew the curtains and turned the ceiling lights on, then tried a door which apparently led to a closet in one corner of the room. It was locked. A highboy by the fireplace served to conceal a compact bar.

Sybella went through the archway and lit another lamp, then put out the lights in the living room. The alcove was furnished with a day bed, a kidney desk, and two deep chairs. A built-in bookcase held two china cats which regarded her haughtily from their perch on the top shelf. Several mysteries and current best sellers, still in their jackets, added a touch of riotous color.

Over the kidney desk hung a round mirror in an ornate gilt frame. Set in a circle around the edge of its convex surface were a score or more of tinier round mirrors, about the size of quarters. The whole thing picked up the contents of the room in toto and tossed it back at Sybella in a confusion of miniature pictures, scrupulous in detail, but incalculably small. As she sat down at the desk, she found it disturbing to see herself multiplied so many times and reduced to elfin proportions. The lilliputian troup of Sybellas aped her mockingly as she opened the drawer.

It contained blotting paper, pens and stationery, and a copy of the *New Yorker,* dated several months before. Uninteresting, at best, Sybella decided, as she closed it.

She got up and surveyed the books on the shelves, but there was certainly nothing there.

"—what she kept and what she threw away—"

She returned to the desk and opened the drawer once more. There were two *New Yorkers* instead of one as she had thought at first. They were dated a week apart and each one had the corner of a page turned down. At least they were something Troy had kept. Sybella opened the first one at the place which was marked, then spread it flat on the desk and opened the second. Together they formed two parts of a profile of Daniel Pine.

There were clippings too, tucked in the back of the second issue; many clippings cut haphazardly from papers of different dates.

Lost in her task, Sybella spread them out in neat array on the desk top and began to read.

The first was about a widow named Cornelia Brown, who had

two sons. One had been killed in action, and only that day the other had been run over by a taxi. The second clipping concerned a sergeant named Felix Nightingale who had come to New York on four days leave to be married and become separated from his bride during their first ten minutes in town.

She pored through still more clippings and her confusion heightened as she read along.

An elderly suicide in a cheap hotel. A man found beaten half to death beside a railroad siding. An aviator killed on his first test flight. Three undernourished children taken from drunken parents by the Children's Aid.

"—what she kept—"

Clipping after clipping full of human misery, shoved in the back of a magazine containing the profile of Daniel Pine.

Searching inspiration she looked up into the mocking mirror and saw that the twenty locked doors to the twenty closets in the twenty rooms behind her were all standing open. She realized then that twenty times over she had been very careless and tried to scream, but really never had time.

3

There were moments when Duncan Maclain waged a silent bitter battle against loneliness. The moments had become more frequent since his partner, Spud Savage, was called to Washington. After his dinner with Lucia and Sybella, he faced with distaste the return to his penthouse knowing that Rena was away.

Sybella's abrupt departure had piqued him a trifle but during the year he had known her it had been a point of honor with him never to pin her down about appointments, or whether she wanted to go or stay. It was true that he rigorously demanded the same consideration in return, so when Sybella suggested after dinner that her stock was in the process of being inventoried, the Captain failed to connect it with their earlier conversation and had nothing to say.

"The amusements of a blind man are limited," he said to Lucia over the coffee and green Chartreuse. "Would you like to hear some talking books? I have a new shipment that just arrived today."

"I'd love it," she told him frankly. "There isn't much pleasure in returning to a room in a big hotel."

"Well, come along." The Captain paid the check and rose with a smile. "You'll be compromised, of course, visiting a bachelor's penthouse on Saturday night."

"Delightful," said Lucia. "Chaperons always bored me."

"Don't worry, we'll have plenty." The Captain took her arm as they went through the lobby. "We'll get a taxi outside. It'll make it easier for our collection of shadows to stick to the trail."

He skipped from one subject to another on the ride through Central Park, steering adroitly away from the topic of Larmar in jail, and skillfully managed to raise Lucia's confidence to a point where she felt his efforts to free her husband could not fail.

The desk clerk delivered a message as they entered the Captain's apartment hotel.

"A man was here to see you, Captain Maclain." The clerk consulted the slip. "A fellow by the name of Mitchell. He wanted to talk to you personally but couldn't wait. He said he'd come again."

"Mitchell?" The Captain lifted his brows.

"Brownie," Lucia explained. "Do you think—?"

"Try to keep away from conjectures, Lucia," Maclain said as

they got in the elevator. "They do no good and they're always upsetting."

She agreed with a touch of her fingers on his arm.

"I must be losing my grip," he continued softly. "Everyone calls Mitchell "Brownie," and his real name meant nothing to me at all."

The boy let them off at the twenty-fourth floor where they changed to a smaller push-button lift that took them to the penthouse.

Lucia found that the office looked different, and decided it was because she had only seen it by daylight before. At night it was lighted softly from hidden vapor tubes concealed in the paneled walls.

She seated herself in the deep leather chair facing the Captain's desk, then got up suddenly without explanation and moved to the broad divan along the wall.

Lucia watched in silence as he slid back a panel and filled two tiny cordial glasses from a bottle he took from the bar.

"There's something disquieting about your accuracy, Captain," Lucia remarked as she took the glass from his hand. "You pick out green Chartreuse without hesitation and fill two little glasses almost to the brim without spilling a drop."

"I can also go to the kitchen and pick out any kind of soup from a large assortment of cans." His face lighted up. "You're in a blind man's home, Lucia, and you've paid a very great tribute to the marvelous people who keep my life in order. I can find anything in this penthouse because the smallest object has its place and is never moved. I always know where things are."

"Don't tell me you can cook!"

"Rather better than average," said Duncan Maclain. "I open cans with a patented opener screwed to the wall. Saucepans are hung in a row close to hand. The range is electric. Merely by feeling the position of the knobs I can tell which burners are off and on, and how high. I've made dough and pastry." He grinned. "There was an almighty mess around Sarah's kitchen, but I had to prove to myself that I could do it. Today, believe it or not, I can bake a very creditable pie."

"And filling the glasses?" Lucia asked. "How can you tell when they're full?"

"Timing," said Duncan Maclain. "You get used to it over a period of years. Then, I have a little trick which may offend you as a hostess. I keep one finger close to the mouth of the bottle and I can tell when the liquid starts to pour. With high-ball glasses the ice comes up to the top, and you can feel it easily when the glass is full. You might shut your eyes and experiment sometime, but I'd advise you to have a linoleum floor when you try."

He sat down at his desk and rapidly dialed the phone. "I want to get the number of William Brown Mitchell who lives above his gun shop." He gave the address, and added, "I'd be very glad to look it up in the phone book, but I'm blind."

After a moment he pressed down the bar and dialed again.

"No answer, Lucia. Later on I'll give him another try."

He was silent for so long that Lucia finally said, "What about your books?"

The Captain left his desk and went to another cabinet in the wall. He took out a square black case labeled in large white letters in the upper right hand corner:

U. S. MAIL

FREE

Sound Reproduction

Records For The Blind

Underneath in even larger letters was the warning:

FRAGILE
PROPERTY OF
U. S. GOVERNMENT
(LIBRARY OF CONGRESS)

Concealed in another section of the cabinet was a squat black reproducer.

The Captain took a record from the case, touched one side with his fingers, then held it out so Lucia could see. "I'm in one of my poetic spells tonight," he explained. "This is *The Rubaiyat* of Omar Khayyam, put into English quatrains by FitzGerald and read by Alexander Scourby. It's a single record. You'll notice the title is in Braille on one side of it."

"Do you have to buy those?" Lucia asked.

He shook his head.

"Both the records and the machine are lent to the blind by the Library of Congress. I just happen to be one of those fortunate enough to have sufficient means to buy my own machine. I have a hookup with my Capehart." He pointed to the large cabinet reproducer close by, then selected a new needle, put it in the sound arm and placed the record on the machine.

Before he started the record he remarked with a touch of bitterness, "This is one of the projects which President Roosevelt put across under the Emergency Relief Act and which the public loves to smugly term boon-doggling. They're inclined to overlook the fact that there are one hundred and twenty thousand blind people in the United States and that only a small proportion of them are able to read Braille. In addition, the blind are given employment in manufacturing, packing and shipping the records and machines."

He started the record and sat down. When *The Rubaiyat* was finished he played a ten record set of Walt Whitman's *Leaves of Grass.*

Lucia was astonished to find it was half past eleven when the last of Whitman's sonorous stanzas died away. She got up and said regretfully, "I'd like to sit here all night long, but I really must be getting home."

The Captain escorted her to the door, and came back in to stand in front of the machine after she had gone. At last he selected another record and carefully put it on. The voice of House Jameson began to recite:

"We have sailed many months, we have sailed many weeks,
  (Four weeks to the month you may mark),
But never as yet ('tis your Captain who speaks)
  Have we caught the least glimpse of a Snark!"

The house telephone rang to announce a visitor. Maclain said, "Send him up," and went back to the talking book machine to replay his favorite verse from *The Hunting of the Snark.*

By the time it had finished, the double chime in the anteroom announced someone at the penthouse door. He stopped the machine and went to let Davis in.

"Hello, Captain. I'm sorry to bust in on you this late." The inspector pushed by and crossed the office to pour himself a long straight Scotch at the open bar.

The Captain stood rigid at the office door as though he might be watching Davis's depredation of the liquor.

"Yes, it is late, Davis," he said after a time. "What's wrong?"

"Maybe I am." The inspector gulped down half his potion and choked a little. "What do you know about this Singleton killing that you're not telling?"

He sat on the arm of a chair and tugged at his clipped mustache, but his hard gray eyes kept looking around the office, stopping on everything except Duncan Maclain.

The Captain walked in slowly and halted almost in the geometrical center of the room. "What do you know about the Singleton killing that *you're* not telling, Davis? There's something in your voice tonight that I've never heard before."

"Christ almighty, Maclain, there's more to this thing than I thought." The inspector bounced up and started to pace the floor, then twisted around suddenly in front of Maclain and seized his arm. "Did you send Sybella Ford up to search that girl's apartment?"

"No." The Captain's mouth was a thin white line.

"Well, somebody got her," said Davis. "She's unconscious in the East River hospital with a fractured skull. A woman in the downstairs apartment heard her fall."

The Captain said, "Yes?" and crossed the room to open the terrace door and step out into the night. When he came back in, his hand was twisted tight in three folds of Dreist's heavy chain.

The inspector drew back before the police dog's unfriendly glare and asked, "What are you going to do with that murderous devil?"

"I'm going to kill somebody with him," said Duncan Maclain. "Come on, let's go."

4

The big police Cadillac streaked across Seventy-second Street and hooted its siren at an adverse red light as it crossed the juncture of Amsterdam Avenue and Broadway.

Dreist sat on the seat at the Captain's right, staring out of the window with an air of unconcern.

Davis lit a cigarette and looked across the Captain at the dog's long, punishing jaw. "Isn't it rather dangerous to take Dreist around a hospital?" he inquired.

"It's dangerous to take him anywhere," said Duncan Maclain. "It's also dangerous to pack a loaded gun."

The inspector flicked ashes on the floor and said in a disgruntled tone, "You might turn him loose in the children's ward and give the kiddies some fun."

"I don't remember mentioning anything about going to a hospital," said Maclain.

"No?" The inspector leaned forward and spoke to the driver. "Pull up to the curb a minute, Alec. We're on the wrong run." He turned back to Maclain. "I thought you'd want to see Sybella."

"You said she was unconscious."

Davis murmured, "Umm."

"I presume you have a man with her."

"Archer's there."

"Then of what use would I be?" asked Maclain. "Tell your driver to head for the Singleton place uptown."

Streets that were dark forever slid by, marked only by the change of the motor's sound and the siren's occasional moan. Davis, who was wiser than most men, kept his steel trap mouth shut tight and let the Captain alone.

It was hot and dark and humid. Dreist showed his sharp white teeth and began to pant. Drops of saliva fell from his lolling tongue. Then he shivered slightly and whimpered at the icy touch of his master's hand.

Streets that were dark forever.

Once Sybella had asked him, "Are you happy in your marriage?"

"I've never been married, Sybella."

"You're married to your dog. How can a man so brilliant be so stupid? You pride yourself that you can see better than a man with eyes, yet you refuse to look at life every day. You, the infallible detective, the man who can shoot at sound to kill—you're afraid, frightened you'll be a burden to some woman who might think it was heaven to have such a burden."

"I'm an infallible god damn fool," the Captain said so loudly that Dreist started.

Davis flicked his cigarette out of the window. "She'll come out of it all right, Captain."

"One way or another," said Duncan Maclain, "I've developed myself into a monstrously clever fellow. My brain's as fertile as a pomegranate. My heart's as cold as Troy Singleton in morgue vault Twenty-two. I do jigsaw puzzles and hook together pieces of wood that I can't even see. It makes a picture of death, Davis. I'm blind Justice, the messenger of God. Stick around with me long enough and I'll get you, too."

"Oh, shut up, for the love of Christ," said Davis. "You're loosening a screw. We're nearly to the apartment. What are you going to do?"

"Lock the stable after the horse is gone," said Duncan Maclain. "God's messenger, me—and you!"

A radio car parked outside had attracted a dozen curious people.

The inspector dismissed it and told a uniformed officer, "Move this bunch of gawkers along."

The helpful old lady who had talked to Sybella met them in the downstairs hall and grew twittery at the sight of Dreist, and Maclain. She stood in their way at the foot of the stairs and kept saying over and over, "That poor young woman. Just imagine! Is there anything I can do?"

"You can go to sleep and get some rest," the inspector said, not unkindly.

He took the Captain's arm and went upstairs beside him, following the tow of Dreist's taut chain. The old lady stood where they had left her, still repeating, "Just imagine!" Finally the Captain heard her go inside her apartment and close the door.

Another uniformed man was waiting in the hall.

The inspector said, "You're relieved. There's nothing more here to hang around for."

The man saluted and clumped downstairs.

The Captain stood to one side clutching Dreist, then followed Davis in. In the sitting room he took off the dog's chain and gave a quiet order in German.

Dreist sat on his haunches, immobile, and Davis muttered, "A Nazi!" and inquired again of the Captain, "Now that you're here, what are you going to do?"

"Give me a picture of the layout," said Duncan Maclain, and started a tour of the room, lightly brushing tables and chairs as he passed and listening to the inspector's succinct descriptions. Once around, he made a second encircling survey, following the wall and hesitating a second at every window and door.

Davis straddled a chair and chewed a toothpick.

Maclain went under the arch and into the alcove.

Finally Davis said, "You're standing right close to where they found her."

"Show me," the Captain ordered.

Davis grunted, then ambled under the archway and stretched himself out on the floor. The Captain stooped and felt the inspector's head, feet and hands.

"Okay."

Davis got up, brushing off his knees.

Maclain sat down at the kidney desk and after a wait said, "What are you looking for?"

"My toothpick," said Davis. "I dropped it playing Oscar the dummy for you on the floor."

Maclain began to toy with the head of a brass key in the kidney desk drawer.

"I'm tired," said Davis.

"It's auto-intoxication from eating too much wood," the Captain told him. "Have you a list of the articles found on Sybella?"

"I always have everything," said Davis, and produced a piece of paper from his pocket. He read off, "In her bag, twenty dollars cash, a gold pencil and notebook, vanity case and lipstick, gold wrist watch not running, eighty-four cents in change in the change purse, handkerchief, shopping list, two opened letters."

"Somebody tried to kill her," said Duncan Maclain. "What for?"

"Maybe he wanted to get out." The inspector put the paper back in his pocket.

"Well, why didn't he get out?" asked the Captain. "What's the matter with the door?"

"Maybe he's the kind of a guy who likes to hit people," said Davis, and chewed his mustache. "Then again maybe he wanted to find out if she had found anything that he had been looking for."

"You wouldn't be admitting, would you, Larry, that this man might have been up here searching for something which would clear Larmar Jordan?"

"No, I wouldn't," said Davis morosely. "You wouldn't be admitting, would you, Captain, that that was what Sybella was looking for?"

"Yes, I would," said Duncan Maclain, "and I think she found it. That's what makes me sore. That bastard who hit her was in the closet, Larry."

"What makes you think that?"

"Let me look over the rest of the place and I'll tell you," said Duncan Maclain.

He got up and took the inspector's arm, and with Dreist sticking close to his side, spent twenty minutes inspecting the bathroom, bedroom and kitchen. In the kitchen he felt the open window and said, "Take a look out there, Larry. Shoot your flashlight around."

The inspector leaned out and said, "Fire escape, with a ladder to the roof made for burglars." He pulled back inside. "That's probably how the man got in."

"I doubt it like hell. I think he had a key to the door, but I think that's how Sybella got in."

"Your bedtime stories interest me, Captain. Tell me more."

"I think the man who hit Sybella had a key to the place," Maclain stated flatly. "I think he knew about this fire escape and opened the window as a means of exit in case someone came to the door. Sybella had no key. Take a look in that waste basket by the kitchen sink, Larry."

"You just got through rummaging around in it," said Davis, but he crossed nevertheless and shined his flashlight in it.

"There are three damp paper towels in there," said Duncan Maclain. "Are they dirty?"

"Very."

"Sybella climbed down by the ladder, got in here and washed her hands in the sink. The man was in the living room and so intent on something that he didn't hear her. As a matter of fact, I don't think he heard her until she was close to the living-room door. There's no place to hide in that living room, Larry, except in the closet. I think he hid in there and took a chance that she wouldn't stay long."

"If she was searching the place, why didn't she find him?" the inspector asked.

"That's an old-fashioned closet," said Duncan Maclain. "It locks with a key. The key's inside the door. I think Sybella found something in that kidney desk that took her a long time, so long that the man in the closet got nervous. I think—" He reached down to put a hand on Dreist who had stiffened at his knee, then lowering his voice, "I think we may have trouble, Larry. Switch off the light, but don't pull your gun with Dreist around."

"What the hell's the matter now?" asked Davis.

The Captain said, "We've a visitor out in the hall."

As he spoke, Martin Gallagher with a blue thirty-eight held tight in his heavy fist stepped in through the kitchen door.

Dreist drove in like a big brown comet, snaked up sideways, and jumped before the man with the deep cleft chin could raise his arm to fire. An instant later, man and dog were down in a heap on the floor.

"If you move, he'll tear you to pieces," said Duncan Maclain, and spat a quiet order to Dreist.

The dog fell back, his dark eyes moving with terrible malice from the man to the gun beside him on the floor.

"I'll tear you to pieces if you don't get that god damn dog off of me," said Gallagher. "What the hell right have you to be prowling through my wife's apartment? What are you and that copper looking for?"

". . . yet it will come:"

I

"WHAT ABOUT IT, Larry?" the Captain asked, "shall I let him up?"

The inspector grimaced. "He's doing us no good where he is. Maybe he knows something."

Maclain gave the dog a sharp command. Dreist reluctantly backed away from his prisoner and took his post at the Captain's side. The inspector took a step forward and Maclain warned, "Wait! Don't pick up the gun. Slide it near to me where I can get it myself."

The scar on Gallagher's chin glowed red. He watched with silent animosity as the inspector used one foot to push the revolver closer to Maclain.

Dreist stood rigid, his heavy head moving in an arc to follow the course of the gun.

The Captain leaned over, picked up the revolver and put it in his pocket. "You'd better give him a once-over, Larry. He may have another."

Gallagher said, "Who do you think you've captured, Billy the Kid?" He started to get to his knees.

"Stay where you are, Gallagher," Maclain ordered sharply. "I presume you are Gallagher, since you're married to Troy."

The hair ruffled up on Dreist's neck at his master's tone.

Gallagher complaisantly relaxed and made no move at the inspector's adroit search.

"Okay, let him up," said Davis.

Maclain signaled the police dog into inactivity by holding one hand palm down.

Gallagher got up slowly, rubbing his arm and eyeing the place where Dreist's teeth had ripped the cloth of his blue serge coat. "The law works both ways," he announced with ill-suppressed anger. "I've a permit for that gun and I have a right to use it in defense of my home."

"You've been reading too many books," Davis told him. "Right now you have the permit, but we have the gun. Let's go into the living room and sit down. We're interested in your home."

"I might add," the Captain put in, "the dog's very effective at stopping a man who tries to run."

"I came up here to find out something," said Gallagher, as they moved off down the hall. "You've nothing on me. I don't need to run."

"So you came up here to find out something?" asked Davis as they reached the living room and sat down. "It's a pity your wife wasn't home this evening to entertain the visitors. She'd have had a lot of fun. How did you get in?"

Gallagher crossed his legs and glared about the carefully appointed room. "Through the door. You left it open. What do you mean there's been a lot of visitors?"

"I take a cop off the door at six o'clock tonight and everybody in New York drops in." He located a toothpick and said, "Let's decide right now who's going to talk first. We turned you loose this morning, but I'm getting a bit sick of your showing up places. You're too damn cocky and it gripes me. Who came here with you?"

"Nobody," said Gallagher, "not even your shadow. I shook him downtown."

The inspector muttered, "Some fun!" and said louder, "I don't know what you're up to, Gallagher, but you're not helping things by your attitude nor by packing a gun."

"Yeah?" Gallagher squared his shoulders and uncrossed his legs and leaned belligerently forward. "It isn't of much interest to the department, I know, but I'm trying to find my wife's murderer. That's reason enough for packing a gun."

The Captain reached down and closed a hand on Dreist's collar. "You seem to be laboring under the same delusion that I am, Mr. Gallagher. The delusion that Troy Singleton's murderer is running around New York. Inspector Davis assures me that he's safely tucked away in jail."

"That's where he'll stay," said Davis, "until you turn up something better."

There was a speculative glint in Gallagher's metallic eyes as he turned from Davis and focused on Maclain. "Where the hell do you fit in this picture, Mister?" he demanded after an instant's study of the Captain. "You're blind as a bat, aren't you?"

The Captain nodded agreement.

Gallagher snapped out abruptly, "Well, what's your game?"

Davis said, "The party's becoming right chummy from what I can see. Maybe I'd better introduce you two. He's a private investigator, Gallagher. Captain Duncan Maclain."

"I know who he is," said Gallagher. "I want to know what's his game."

"For the moment, it seems to be the same as yours. Maybe we'd better get together," said Maclain.

"If you think you're going to trick me into talking, you're crazy." Gallagher set his jaw. "I'm playing a lone hand."

"Maybe that's the trouble," the Captain suggested with a smile that had no amusement behind it. "Too many of us are playing a lone hand. We seem to be getting in each other's way." He raised his expressive eyebrows and turned his head to include the grim inspector. "There have been several cases where Duncan Maclain and the Homicide Squad worked together with excellent results. That, of course, was back in other days."

"Other days, hell," said Davis, snapping his toothpick between his teeth. "You're worse than Minnie the Moocher, Maclain, when you want to get your own way." He took the broken half of the toothpick from his mouth and examined it unhappily. "I couldn't get Larmar Jordan out of jail if I wanted to. The case has passed into the hands of the D. A."

"He's safer there, anyway," the Captain remarked.

"Safer from what?" asked Davis.

"Killing."

Davis got up and walked into the hall to try the outside door. Back again, he said, "Now look here, Maclain—"

"Killing," the Captain reiterated calmly. "By the same person who tried to kill him the other day."

"You've let Sybella's accident turn your head."

The Captain's face became a gargoylish mask. "If being hit over the head with a blackjack is an accident, Davis, I've nothing more to say."

The inspector made quick amends. "I didn't mean it like that, Maclain, and you know it. But I don't get what you're driving at about someone trying to kill Larmar. He and the girl were alone there on Thursday."

There was a noise as Gallagher's thick tongue came out and moistened his heavy lips. "Maybe you and I could get together at that, Mister. I don't happen to think that this Jordan guy killed her either. That's what's been driving me on."

"It will make good headlines if it ever gets printed," said Davis. "'Ex-flatfoot Penetrates Penthouse Puzzle'."

"If the Inspector will keep out of this for just five minutes," Gallagher's raspy voice requested, "maybe I'll tell you what brought me here tonight, and maybe I won't. It depends on what you have to say."

The Captain locked his hands behind his head and said, "I understand you've been in the Army, Mr. Gallagher."

"Yes."

"Did you ever hear of exploding a mine by remote control?"

"Yes."

"I believe that the gun that killed your wife was fired in some such way."

Davis made a noise with his lips, and said, "Sleep tight, little kiddies. Uncle Don will be back tomorrow afternoon."

The Captain was unperturbed. "She was shot just as the church chimes began to ring, killed with a hair trigger gun." He leaned back languidly in his chair. "I'd like to draw you a picture. There's a hedge and a terrace wall in back of me, and a desk in front of me. I'm on a terrace, and I have set hours. I work here every day. Somebody has decided to kill me."

The inspector let his interest get the better of him and asked, "Why?"

The Captain closed his perfect, sightless eyes. "Maybe my accounts are short. Maybe somebody has looted my gun collection. Maybe some of my work's been sold and hasn't been reported, and the funds have been misappropriated. Maybe I have a jealous wife or maybe some woman I'm running around with has a jealous lover or husband. Or maybe I'm about to throw over some woman I'm running around with."

"Maybe I'm nuts," said Davis.

The Captain refrained from nodding his head, and continued stolidly. "A thousand other maybes, Larry. One of them might have reached fruition. Who can say?"

"Take the last one," said Gallagher. "I know a dame who had a temper like a hellcat. If a man had attempted to throw her over —" He stopped and left his statement hanging in mid-air.

"Very well, we'll take the last one," said Duncan Maclain. "It's as good as any. I'll tell a bedtime story to your kiddies, Larry. Larmar Jordan was running around with a woman. He got tired of her and told her so one day. She had a friend in Jordan's household and she played on his sympathy and got him to write her a note inviting her to a party."

"Why?" asked Davis.

The Captain shrugged. "In the event that anybody might question her about being around the Jordans' apartment, she'd have something to show and something to say. She was mad—a temper like a hellcat. Also she was clever. Strangely enough she knew quite a lot about guns."

"What guns?" demanded Gallagher.

"Guns that were worth money," said Duncan Maclain and spread out his hands. "Once when Jordan was in a financial hole, she sold one for him to a man named Daniel Pine and got double the money Jordan could have gotten himself."

"Where the hell did you find that out?" asked Davis.

"I'm telling the kiddies a bedtime story," said Duncan Maclain. "You mustn't take my bedtime story seriously, Larry. It goes against the grain. This woman not only learned about expensive guns, she learned about guns that could kill. She wrapped one up in a handkerchief and wedged it into the terrace wall in back of where I'm sitting." He jerked a thumb over his shoulder. "You will remember that for the moment I'm Larmar Jordan, the writer, and I work here every day."

"And what was supposed to fire it?" Davis demanded.

"Vibration of some kind," said the Captain.

"Oh, you've come back to the carillon again."

The Captain slowly shook his head. "Not if my bedtime story's true, Davis. The carillon was something this clever lady never counted on. Certainly, if she'd known the carillon was to discharge that pistol at exactly a quarter to six with Larmar Jordan away from his desk and nobody there to stop the bullet, she'd never have seated herself directly in its path."

"Unless it was suicide," said Gallagher stonily.

Maclain slowly opened his eyes. "By God, Davis, there's a sweet idea. Suicide—plus an attempt to kill the man who jilted her by seating him in the electric chair. But this is a bedtime story, Mr. Gallagher, and the pretty heroine is down in the morgue. I'm afraid that she's the only one that could tell us." His ruminations moved to the present. "But you could tell us why you came here tonight."

"I'm trying to find out who she lived with," said Gallagher.

"Unfortunately, you're a little late." There was a break in the Captain's voice. "Though we still may be able to work together." He stood up and said, "You might run me down to the hospital, Davis."

"You can come along too, Gallagher." The inspector began to put out lights.

The Captain fastened the chain on Dreist and walked out ahead of the others. He rode in somber silence on the trip downtown.

At the hospital Davis found the doctor and waited outside the door of Sybella's room.

Maclain spoke softly to the surgeon and went in, leaning on the doctor's arm.

Sybella was still unconscious and for an instant his sensitive fingers touched her hand against the counterpane.

"What?" asked Davis when the Captain reappeared.

"Nothing," said Duncan Maclain.

2

Sunday it rained.

Up early, the Captain dawdled over his breakfast. He couldn't see the lack of sun, but he still reacted strongly to the moisture-laden atmosphere of the depressing day.

Sarah Marsh, his cook, looked at him reproachfully as he pushed aside his second cup of coffee and stalked from the dining room into his office.

For an hour he sat twiddling with a jigsaw puzzle which refused to fit. Usually the pieces were alive to Duncan Maclain. Today they seemed nothing more than insensate, challenging pieces of wood cut into enigmatic designs by some workman who maliciously wished to annoy him. For the first time in many years, his fingers were fumbling thumbs.

An agitating ferocity crept over him as he strove to put the malignant pieces together. Finally it vented itself in a quick display of anger. Seizing one piece larger than the rest between his powerful fingers, the Captain snapped it in two as though it were a fragment of goldfish food, and tossed the halves away. They struck on the heavy rug in the middle of the room and he quieted at the sound of their fall. After a moment he left his desk and found them again.

Working with the intensity of a jeweler setting a diamond, he located a tube of glue in his drawer, delicately fitted the broken halves and glued them together. They stuck, but the wood would never be whole again. The process had left a scar. He put the mended fragment in an ash tray to dry and restored the other pieces to their box.

His face was ravaged with some great internal upheaval as he selected a record haphazardly, put it on the Capehart, and started it playing.

Back at his desk, he sat immobile with his hands quiescent, a dangerous symptom in a man who lived through the assiduous touch of his fingers.

The music failed to register. The record gave forth notes and scales, blared with brass, and sighed with strings. A singer breathed and raised his voice with feeling. The record stopped.

It left the room too silent.

The messenger of God.

' The lives of people who lived and breathed and loved and hated had dropped down into a deep black pit of anonymity. Marriages, births, and deaths were not vital statistics; they were pieces of a puzzle.

You didn't kiss a woman's lips because you loved her and wanted to marry her. You kissed her lips to bolster your *amour propre* by her sweet response. You could use her to solve your puzzles, and puzzles correctly solved proved how good you were. What difference if she loved you and you snapped her life in two between your clever fingers?

"Damn life to hell, anyhow," said Duncan Maclain.

He had discovered something that could not be broken and mended again with the sticky glue of self-esteem. Happiness had been quite close and he'd stubbornly refused to touch it.

His seldom absent touch of humor deserted his rugged face and left it ugly.

He had one more job to do. The reward was enough to keep him going although it consisted only of bringing a little happiness to a couple of people he liked. Beyond that, there wasn't much left except the cloying taste of that sweetish poison known as revenge.

He sat up with a start and jerkily dialed the phone as though he'd wakened to action from some wildly disturbing dream.

"Ferguson?" he asked when the ringing was answered.

Larmar's lawyer gave a sleepy, "Yes. You woke me up. Sunday's my day to sleep."

"I just woke myself up," said Duncan Maclain. "I have to talk to Jordan today. Can you go down there with me and get me in?"

"What's up?" the attorney demanded more alertly.

"Last night I told Davis a bedtime story and gave myself a new idea."

"About the carillon?" Jess Ferguson was eager now.

"About the carillon," the Captain repeated. "First I have to prove it didn't kill her."

"That'll be helpful," the lawyer disappointedly cut in.

"I have to prove that it didn't kill her before I can prove that it did," said Duncan Maclain. "It's a peculiar situation, Ferguson, in which I know the truth, and yet things are not always what they seem."

It was damp in the visitors' room at the jail. The drizzle outside seemed to have scotched the heavy walls and dissolved them in mistiness until the prison and the outside world merged gloomily together. Even Larmar's voice seemed gray. The Captain found it difficult to force cheerfulness. He sat at the plain board table with Ferguson beside him, and Larmar across from them on a stiff kitchen chair.

It might have been helpful if Larmar had been antagonistic, or anything except apathetic. It was hard to give aid to a man who didn't care. Ferguson grew restive under his client's lack of co-operation, but the Captain persisted gently in his search for information. He seemed to understand better than the lawyer that a man's perception and reactions might be dulled by drabness in a few days of the prison's noisome sanitary smell.

Ferguson broke out angrily. "Maclain's not trying to heckle you, Larmar. He's trying to find out what happened on Thursday. Not part of it. Everything."

"I've told the police," said Larmar, "everything I have to tell."

"It's not enough," said Ferguson. "You're acting like an angry kid. You're the only one who can help yourself right now. If you don't do it, you'll rot right here in this cell."

"I'm rotting anyhow," said Larmar. "What the hell!"

The Captain took out a linen handkerchief and put it to his nose. It felt cool, and he slowly inhaled the scent of the freshly laundered linen. "We've been all over what you told the police, Larmar. I think somebody set a death trap for you."

"You've said that before."

"Nothing you've told the police or me has changed my opinion. I think that the bullet that was meant for you killed Troy."

"I think you're crazy," said Larmar. "I think it's one of Ferguson's wild ideas. It would do nothing but prejudice me, if I was on the jury."

"You're in the prisoner's box," said Duncan Maclain with sudden coldness. "Follow a course of stubborn silence and you'll come out of the prisoner's box with a conviction hung on you for murdering Troy."

"I've told them the truth," said Larmar. "It's up to Ferguson to make it stick."

"A combination of Portia and the late Mr. Fallon couldn't make the truth stick in this case, Larmar." Jess Ferguson turned on the full persuasive powers of his musical voice, and feverishly rumpled his hair. "We need more of the truth, not less." He pulled his chair up closer to his client. "Don't you see, Larmar, if that gun was really fixed in the terrace wall as the Captain claims, somebody had to put it there."

"It's a fool idea I tell you, Ferguson."

"I don't think you really believe that, Larmar," said Duncan Maclain. "I think you're afraid."

"I have a right to be."

"Not for yourself." The Captain leaned back in his chair. "I think you're afraid that your own wife tried to murder you."

"I've had enough of this." Larmar got to his feet with a noisy scrape of his chair.

Ferguson stepped in quickly, conscious that the Captain had struck a vital note. "The easiest way to clear your mind of that silly idea is to answer the Captain's questions if you care anything about Lucia at all. The best way to help her is to start at a point twenty-four hours before the shooting and tell us everybody who was there."

Larmar jerkily resumed his seat.

"On Wednesday night Paul and Brownie Mitchell were there. Lucia and I went to a show and afterward met Bob Morse at a night club. I had too much to drink. She danced with Morse and I got mad and went home."

The Captain said, "Let's take the following day."

"I went up to my agent's in the morning, and came home about one. Morse had lunch with me and we talked about the profile. He said he'd come back in the evening."

The Captain asked, "Did Bob Morse do the profile on Daniel Pine?"

"Yes," said Larmar cautiously. "Why?"

The Captain stroked his upper lip with a finger. "I talked to Pine yesterday. I thought perhaps Bob Morse told you that Daniel Pine might be a good market for your Harpers Ferry gun."

"I have no intention of selling it," said Larmar.

"No, not the one you have now," the Captain told him. "It's a forgery made up for you by Brownie. The date's been filed and changed. Pine's already bought your gun."

Larmar's feet scuffled uneasily underneath the table. "Is that what he told you?"

"Quite inadvertently," said Duncan Maclain. "As a matter of fact, he refused to tell me where he got his Harpers Ferry pistol. Gun collectors are usually quite proud of their source of supply. Your gun was gone. You had covered up its sale to the casual observer by substituting a very clever forgery. Pine wouldn't say where he got his, which left me no alternative but to reach the conclusion that he'd purchased it from Troy."

Larmar closed his eyes and clasped his forehead between his palms. "What the devil has that got to do with anything?"

"Indirectly," said Duncan Maclain, "it caused the death of Troy."

3

Martin Gallagher was a taciturn man with a better education than appeared on the surface. He had one great failing—his inability to divorce himself from a fixed idea. He believed that an individual could order or regulate his own life and existence without the help of society.

While he liked security, he disliked capitalism and seethed against it, fostering all the resentment of a one-track mind. He was a straight line man of action. This combination had led him to join the police force for a time, and he had worked without much imagination, on the side of the law. The Army suited him even better. His love of belligerence carved out a good record for him in the war.

It was the strong attraction of opposites that tricked him into a marriage with Troy. He won her by wearing persistence, for long sustained effort at anything had always been boring to Troy. She had found that life was much easier if one held out to a point of being annoyed, then quietly succumbed.

Once he had her, he damned her to perdition and loved her to distraction, for every trait absent in Martin Gallagher was present a hundredfold in Troy. He was a bulldog mated to a French poodle who knew every trick of attraction and loved nothing so much as the diamond collar about her neck and the cut of her beautiful hair.

Nevertheless, she was Gallagher's in the eyes of the church and the law, and like the bulldog, once he had something, Martin Gallagher knew how to hang on with tooth and jaw.

He had no illusions about her, for he wasn't a fool. From the day of their marriage, Troy had fussed and fumed and double-crossed him to get the things which couldn't be bought on the modest salary of a representative of the law.

In the Army and away from her, Gallagher knew she'd run hog-wild. Still, the main thing that sustained him as a soldier was the thought of getting back to Troy. When he returned to find her dead, her mean little traits were wiped from his mind, leaving only a longing built up through lonely nights and endless days. Martin Gallagher became a nemesis; a simple, high tempered man robbed of his most prized possession, living a life which was robbed of its only joy.

He went to work, with the unending patience and brash un-imaginativeness of an ex-policeman, to question everyone who had ever been connected with the murdered girl. In this he knew much more than either Duncan Maclain or the New York police, for he knew her past life, which she had covered with care. Unfortunately, he had no desire whatsoever to help Larmar Jordan or further justice. Death was his goal. A bullet for a bullet.

When he got up Sunday morning and stared from the window of his cheap hotel at the rain-soaked roofs of the city, he felt he was nearing the end of the trail.

Ordinarily brusque and forthright, depending on the sledge hammer qualities of his questions, he had developed a certain amount of caution from his interviews with Lucia and Daniel Pine. From them he had learned nothing except what his experience on the police force should have taught him: that when you were trying to get information about a murder, it was better to go slowly.

People were scared of murder. A simple demand for the truth shut them up completely, or what was worse, started them lying even when it could not hurt them to tell you what you wanted to know.

Gallagher had not liked his interview at headquarters. They had grilled him plenty. Equally, he had not liked busting into Troy's apartment and getting tangled up with the blind man's dog. The blind man was smart, too smart for a man who was playing a lone hand and hunting for revenge. It had taught him one thing though; that the blind man was on the side of the law, and better avoided.

Well, he still had a couple more calls to make, but he intended to play his cards close to his chest. By the end of this dismal Sunday, he should know.

He had breakfast in a lunchroom near his hotel, and when he was finished, made a telephone call. The result was satisfactory.

Heedless of the rain which rapidly soaked his blue serge coat, shrinking it even closer, he walked east to Fifth Avenue and caught a bus downtown. A short time later he rang the bell of the Jordans' apartment.

The door was opened by Paul.

Gallagher asked, "Are you the man I spoke to on the phone?"

"Yes. Come in," said Paul.

Gallagher walked into the room where he had talked with Lucia on Friday night and sat down.

Paul's sharp black eyes followed the broad wet shoulders. It was early to start drinking, but Paul poured out two straight Scotches at the bar, took them into the living room with him and set one beside Gallagher.

Gallagher said, "I never touch the stuff," and pushed the glass to one side.

"Good, I'll drink it myself," said Paul.

He took the whisky with him to the couch and swallowed it neat before he sat down.

Gallagher said, "As I told you over the telephone, I think I can clear Jordan, if you'll give me some information about my wife."

"Why don't you go to the police?" asked Paul.

Gallagher's red face was a blank. "They've got a man. What the hell would they want to clear him for?"

"I get it. What do you want to know?" asked Paul.

Gallagher touched the scar on his chin. "I've been on 'the police force, myself."

"So I've heard."

"I've been in the Army and the Merchant Marine."

"Go on," said Paul.

"I found out the only way to get answers to questions is to ask them."

"Well, why don't you ask them?"

"Because you told me you'd be here by yourself." He pointed a heavy finger to the door of Lucia's room. "Is there somebody in there or isn't there? Don't try to stall."

"There's a friend of mine named Morse in there," said Paul. "If you think I'm going to get myself tied up in a confidential talk with you, Gallagher, you're crazy. I think you're dangerous."

"For all of me," said Gallagher, "Jordan can stay in jail and spoil. I'm going."

The bedroom door opened and Bob Morse came out, his round face serious. "Wait a minute, Mr. Gallagher. I've run across quite a few of your late wife's escapades. What's the matter with asking us both about what you want to know?"

"I don't trust snooping reporters," said Gallagher.

"From what I can see you don't trust anybody," said Paul.

Bob said, "Get me a drink, Paul, will you? A big one." He stepped in front of Gallagher barring his progress toward the door. "You're not going to get any place with your temper, Mr. Gallagher. I don't print anything anybody asks me not to. If you can do anything to get Larmar Jordan out of jail, I'll give you all the information you want, and so will Paul. Now, sit down and keep your shirt on, and act like a human being. You'll gain nothing by getting yourself into a boil."

For a second Gallagher's face looked mean, then he settled

himself down into the chair again as Paul came back from the bar.

Bob took his highball and eased his weight on the arm of a chair.

"Well, what makes now?" asked Paul.

"I want to know who introduced my wife to Larmar Jordan," said Gallagher slowly.

"I did," said Paul.

Gallagher puckered his lips and relaxed them again, and blood glowed red in his scar. "Where?"

"At a cocktail party about a year ago," said Paul.

"Who gave the party?"

Paul thought a minute. "Hawkins, or something. She lives on West Twelfth Street and her husband's a war correspondent. What difference does it make?"

Gallagher sat biting on his thumb nail. "She was living with some man while I was away. Bought him clothes and presents. She kept it damn good and quiet, but I've talked to storekeepers up around her place, and they've seen her in there with a fellow."

"The same fellow?" asked Bob.

Gallagher turned on him, his face ferocious. "You print that and I'll knock your head off."

"He's not going to print it," Paul stuck in quickly.

"If it was the same man she was in there with, it might mean something. If she was in there with different men, you should have sense enough to know it means nothing at all."

"I intend to find out," said Gallagher, turning back to Paul, and growing crafty. "Do you think Jordan would know who she'd been living with?"

Paul shook his head. "He'd have quit her cold. He's not a wolf."

"He might have known," Gallagher persisted. "She could make a man do funny things." He leaned a little closer. "Jordan might talk to save himself if you put it to him right."

"I'm not going to put it to him," said Paul.

Gallagher turned to Bob. "What do you know about her?"

"Nothing good," said Bob with a scowl. "I know she got money out of Larmar, and maybe some from Daniel Pine. I know there must have been others."

"What others?" Gallagher snapped. "If you know, you know their names."

Bob took a long pull on his drink and said, "God, you're touchy. A girl like that always has others. It takes practice to work men like Larmar and Daniel Pine."

Gallagher got up slowly. "You haven't told me anything I didn't already know."

"That's tough," said Paul. "If it's any help to you, I remember who invited me to that Hawkins' party on Twelfth Street."

"Who?" asked Gallagher.

"It was Larmar's agent."

"What's his name," asked Gallagher.

"It's a her," said Paul. "Sarah Hanley."

Gallagher picked up his hat from the chair. "You still haven't told me anything. I was going to talk to Sarah Hanley anyhow. Before my wife got fancy, Sarah used to be a friend of hers and mine."

"You'll find her at the St. Regis Hotel," said Paul.

4

There had been many footsteps in the life of Duncan Maclain. He had never paid much attention to them during the twenty years of his existence prior to the first World War. Those of his mother and father had become familiar during his early years, and were something to look forward to. Then they had silenced, and life had gone on.

There had been the light footsteps of a girl or two, and one in particular. He had lost them somehow when blindness struck him during the war.

It was curious how time and his own efforts had dimmed the memory of things he once could see. Deprived of sight, he entered a new world and took up a new existence, mastering it letter by letter and precept upon precept, like a child who has just been born.

Footsteps became important, to be classed with laughter and tone of voice and length of stride, and other invisible means of perception which Duncan Maclain considered necessary to his progress on an unseen sphere.

Like voices, footsteps became people. Tie up footsteps, laughter, and tone of voice, and you have an individual's name. The footsteps were probably more important than the voice and laughter, for you could hear them a long way off and tell before the owner approached you whether he or she was fat or thin, or short or tall. After some years of listening, your acumen might be sharpened to a point where the footsteps revealed the owner's state of mind.

There were footsteps bright and excited, and the footsteps of hopelessness which were laggard and dull. You might even learn to tell policemen, or the hasty upset progress of a fugitive, or the man who for years had paced a cell by the way he walked on a six by nine rug in your room. Undoubtedly, footsteps were valuable things to a blind man, but they might also be something to worry about.

Since he had involved himself in the Jordans' troubles, several different sets of footsteps had attached themselves to Duncan Maclain. At different times they had changed. When he had taken a taxi, they had transposed themselves neatly into the noise of a following car. He began to find them comforting, over and above the annoyance, for they spelled a kind of safety. After a couple of days, he was even able to distinguish the highly efficient ones which marked a member of the police department from the slightly more artful tread of the operators employed by Daniel Pine.

Sunday morning, taking Schnucke for an early walk before breakfast, he found that both sets of footsteps had gone. Then, almost imperceptibly, another set came into his life, a set that was furtive and fearfully careful. He sensed them first when he left the visitors' room in the Tombs with Ferguson after their visit to Larmar.

"Someone following us?" he asked the lawyer.

Ferguson turned around. "I don't see anyone."

"I guess I'm shying at echoes," said Maclain.

But the echoes were not his own or the lawyer's, and he knew it. He and Ferguson were not moving along on tiptoe, taking pains not to be seen. The Captain decided that the owner of the footsteps was safely hidden in some angle of the hall. Outside, waiting in the drizzle for a taxi, he decided he might have been mistaken.

A cab pulled up and jolted them off on the journey uptown. Maclain turned part of his attention from Ferguson's comments to sort out the noise of a following motor, but could hear none.

He dropped the lawyer at his Park Avenue apartment, and continued alone uptown.

Two messages were waiting, one to call Paul, and another from Sarah Hanley. He telephoned Paul first.

Paul said, "Brownie's been trying to get ahold of you and you were out."

"I missed him, too."

"He's been trying a few experiments. He told me you thought that Stotzer pistol might have been fired by vibration."

"And what were the experiments?" asked Maclain.

"He found out that if you have the rate of vibration, a hair trigger pistol might be fired by church chimes or a siren or nearly anything. He says if you'll go to his shop at eight o'clock tonight, he'll show you. Morse will be there, too. He thought he might get an angle for a story."

The Captain said, "I think I'll bring Davis and Archer."

Paul hesitated. "Do you think it's wise? Most of those gun-smiths don't want to get mixed up with the police."

"He'll probably get *them* mixed up, which is worse. But if this is going to be of any help, I'd like them to see it themselves. After all, Paul, he'll only be showing them something I've already told them, and he'll only be proving something to me that I already know. Brownie has a nice idea, but it isn't going to get Larmar out of jail unless we can prove that the murderer had a radio station concealed somewhere in the hall."

"Well, I'll tell him you'll be there, anyhow," said Paul.

The Captain hung up and gave Sarah Hanley a call.

"How's Sybella?" the agent demanded. "Any better?"

"I haven't heard." The Captain took a cigarette from the cloisonné box on his desk and lit it. "The hospital's to ring me immediately if there's any change."

"Lucia's coming up for cocktails. Can you join us in about an hour? I'd really like to talk to you, Captain Maclain."

"Who else will be there?"

"Just Lucia and Paul."

"I'll come," said Maclain. He cradled the phone very gently and touched a button on his desk summoning Cappo.

He could hear the buzzer in the kitchen, but nobody answered. Evidently Sarah Marsh and her husband were out for the afternoon.

He got up quietly and brought in Dreist from his kennel on the terrace, then took the chain from Dreist's collar and gave him a low voice order to search.

The powerful dog moved off in speedy silence, nosing open the office door which stood slightly ajar.

Maclain stood still and listened, following the sound of Dreist's search of the dining room, kitchen and servants' quarters. He heard the dog return and pause before the bedroom door, then scurry off downstairs to the lower floor. The Captain knew there was no one in his bedroom or the police dog would have warned him by growling at the door.

He waited a long two minutes until Dreist came up from the lower floor.

It had been imagination then; nerves strung too tight from thinking of Sybella. Imagination was dangerous, like too much emotion. It made you think shadows were trailing you; not police shadows, but the disembodied kind that trod on furtive tiptoe; made you think that guns were fired by shadows.

It was bad to lose your judgment by hearing muffled noises. Terror-stricken women and frightened children heard muffled noises. They trembled under blankets, cowed by a swinging shutter, chilled by a squeaking board or a scurrying mouse.

The only danger to a blind man lay in hearing noises where no noise existed. That meant lack of judgment. Lack of judgment meant death to a man who could not see. It was death to think that in and about your own safe penthouse you had heard a muffled sound.

He took Dreist back to his kennel and firmly closed the terrace door.

The snap of his fingers roused Schnucke from her sleep in the corner. She brought her brace and the Captain snapped it on her. He found his hat and started out, then returned to his desk, stripping off his light gray mohair coat.

A moment later he had buckled on the armpit holster containing his small flat gun. Dressed again, he took a light raincoat from the closet and put it on. Guided by Schnucke's brace, he went through the anteroom and into the penthouse hall, closing and trying the door behind him.

He was on the twenty-sixth floor and must connect with the apartment house elevator on the twenty-fourth. Ten paces straight ahead was the small push button operated lift which would take him down. Now it was coming up, although the Captain had pushed no button.

He walked over quickly beside it, closed a hand warningly over Schnucke's nose and pressed himself back against the wall.

The automatic door slid open, but no one got out. The Captain stayed quite still and waited until the moment when the door would close again of its own volition.

Something came out before it closed, but it wasn't human. It was noise; the noise of cloth as it slithered down against a wall; the noise of a gurgle mingled with a groan.

Schnucke whimpered.

The Captain reached up and pushed the button to hold open the closing door. He knelt outside and reached one long arm in gingerly to feel about the floor of the tiny car.

His hand drew back from the sticky ivory hilt of the dirk in the dead man's stomach, and moved up higher. His fingers touched a face, and a deep cleft chin with a scar.

The automatic door started to close again. The Captain cautiously found a handkerchief and wiped his fingers, then went back into the penthouse and picked up the phone. He called the clerk on the desk downstairs and said, "You'd better see if anyone's trying to get out by way of the staircase. This is Captain Maclain."

He hung up without explaining, dialed police headquarters and finally got Davis on the phone.

"Your ex-policeman, Mr. Gallagher, just rode upstairs in my private elevator with one of Larmar's daggers in his belly, Larry. You'd better turn loose your homicide boys again." He paused an instant. "Tell them to be careful to wipe their feet before they come in my office. There's blood all over the floor of that car."

" . . . the readiness is all."

THE NEW YORK HOMICIDE SQUAD swirled into Duncan Maclain's apartment with the irresistible force and majesty of a
mountainous tidal wave. Through it all, the Captain sat behind
his desk as unaffected as some old man of the sea washed by
frothing water which left him dry.

Davis and Archer arrived as the tide began to recede, and
fixed themselves drinks.

"That was a messy performance if I ever saw one," the inspector said, flopping into a chair.

Sergeant Archer creaked the springs of the leather divan and
remarked, "Gore. I don't like murderers who kill with gore."
He sighed heavily. "But after all, I suppose a knife is much more
quiet than a gun."

The Captain sat with his hands folded on the desk edge, very
aloof and detached from it all.

His attitude began to grate on the inspector who said, "You
were free enough with your theories about the Singleton girl.
Where do you fit this one in?"

"That's your little red wagon, isn't it?" The Captain unfolded
his hands and settled his coat more snugly about his shoulders.

Archer finished his highball and sent out a feeler. "You must
have thought something was going to happen or you wouldn't
be wearing that armpit gun."

"I'd begun to hear things," said Duncan Maclain. "Somebody

started to take an interest in me today, somebody not connected with you or Daniel Pine."

"Gallagher, maybe," Archer suggested and shot a glance at the inspector.

"He didn't need to follow me, Sergeant. Larry heard me tell him last night that it might be a good thing if we worked together. All he needed to do was ring the bell. I'd have been glad to let him in."

Davis said, "Maybe that's what he was trying to do. Get in touch with you, I mean. Of all the rotten cold-blooded—"

"If you're trying to get to the bottom of this second killing, Larry, getting yourself all het up about it isn't the best way to begin."

"We're not trying to get to the bottom of anything," Davis said, aping the Captain's calm. "Archer and I like to ride up and down in elevators full of bodies. We heard about the one you had and thought we'd just drop in."

"I object to your terming this a cold-blooded killing," said Maclain.

Archer asked, "What do you call disembowelment? A warm-blooded killing?"

"I think it was self-defense," said Duncan Maclain.

"Oh, happy day!" The sergeant reached down and scratched his broad shin.

"Self-defense, forsooth." Davis gnawed his mustache and squinted at the Captain. "I'm a little sick of being pushed around, Maclain. This Jordan affair was open and shut until you stepped in. Now you sit there like a bull frog on a lily pad waiting to jump again and stir up more mud in the pool. I've already admitted the case has angles we didn't see at first. But Gallagher's killing isn't one of them. It's pretty damned obvious, isn't it? Somebody was out to get him, followed him up here, and did him in."

"I think you have it backward," said Maclain. "The late Mr. Gallagher was a dangerous man. We returned his gun to him last night. It's just an opinion, of course, but I think Gallagher followed his own killer here with murder in his heart."

"What was the killer doing here?" asked Davis.

"Following me," said Duncan Maclain.

"And how did he get in? Nobody came up in the elevator to the twenty-fourth floor."

"Would you take an elevator under the circumstances?" the Captain inquired mildly. "There are stairs, you know, and a servants' entrance in an alley in the back of the building. I think that's how they both got in. Was Gallagher's gun in his pocket?"

Davis looked at the sergeant, but Archer turned slowly away, refusing to help. After a time the inspector said, "No. It was under him, on the floor."

"Do you like my self-defense idea any better, Larry?"

"No. I don't like it at all, but go ahead, and I'll listen."

"We'll go back to last night. Gallagher said he was going to handle this thing in his own way. Somehow or other, he made up his mind that he'd discovered the person who killed Troy. He followed him here, but he didn't do a very good job of it. Whoever he was trailing was waiting for him on the twenty-fourth floor, probably standing in back of the door to the exit stairs."

"Are you dreaming this up?" Davis demanded.

The Captain shook his head. "I'm trying to reconstruct a picture from very faint noises I heard in the penthouse hall."

"Well, go on and reconstruct," said Davis.

"Gallagher followed his man upstairs, opened the exit door cautiously, and gun in hand, stepped out into the hall. The man in back of the exit door got him from behind, pinned his arms to his sides before he could shoot, and knifed him at the same time. The rush probably carried them close to the lift. The killer pushed the button, opened the door and shoved Mr. Gallagher in. By the time the lift door closed again, he was three or four flights down the stairs."

"And what brought the lift up to your floor?" asked Davis.

"Gallagher," said Maclain. "He wasn't quite gone. To my mind that's about all. I telephoned the desk clerk to have someone watch the stairs as soon as I got in here—before I called you—but the man had gone."

Davis got up and went to inspect the titles of some Braille books ranged along the wall. A man came to the office door, reported to Archer and went away.

The inspector kept his eyes fixed on the books and asked Maclain, "Why was this killer trailing you?"

The Captain countered with, "Why were you?"

"Over a long period of years I've discovered you're a nuisance," said Davis.

"This man's discovered the same thing in a few days. I worry people, Larry. It gets on their nerves trying to predict what a blind man will do." The Captain lifted his shoulders. "Gallagher was predictable. So are you."

"Okay," said Davis, "tell me what I'm going to do."

"You're going to catch this murderer eventually."

"What do you mean eventually?" Archer put in.

"By the time he's killed somebody else," said Duncan Maclain. "You have a certain amount of fixed routine to go through."

"Huh!" said Davis. "And what are you going to do?"

"I'm going to catch him or kill him before he kills anybody else," said Maclain.

The inspector turned around, his gray eyes troubled. "I hope it's not you."

The Captain touched his Braille watch. "I'm going to Sarah Hanley's at the St. Regis for a cocktail, Larry. If you and Archer want to meet me at eight o'clock tonight at Brownie Mitchell's gun shop, you can watch an experiment."

"We're sick of experiments," said Davis. "We've more important things to do."

He nodded to Archer and they moved out in a disapproving parade of two.

The Captain waited a few minutes before he called Schnucke. There were still several men in his penthouse hall. He walked down the two flights of steps to the twenty-fourth floor and caught a house elevator the rest of the way.

Under the canopy he spoke to Mike, the doorman. "Get me a taxi, will you, Mike, and keep your eyes open. I have an idea another cab may follow me."

"If it does, Captain, I'll know."

Mike signaled a taxi after a short delay, and the Captain got in. It was still drizzling.

He stayed alert and on edge during the ride to the St. Regis, but nothing seemed to be following.

Lucia and Paul were in Sarah Hanley's suite and greeted him with brief expressions of sympathy about Sybella. Settled with a cocktail in his hand, the Captain asked idly, "Have you been waiting long?"

Paul said, "I just got here a few minutes ago."

"Martin Gallagher's dead," said Duncan Maclain.

He listened to Lucia's quick gasp of astonishment and Paul Hirst's disbelieving "No!", then told them briefly what had happened.

Lucia asked in a strained voice, "Do you think any of the rest of us are in danger?"

The Captain said, "The police already have a guard on Sybella. If she ever recovers consciousness—"

Lucia said, "She will."

"If she does," the Captain continued without a change of tone, "she may be able to tell us lots of things we'd like to know." He turned to Sarah Hanley. "You can tell me a few right now, if you will."

"What?" The agent seemed slightly flustered as she put her cocktail down.

"I'd like to know what agents do with their clients' money," said Duncan Maclain.

Paul Hirst struck a match and lit a cigarette. Smoke drifted toward the Captain from the other side of the room.

"We deposit it in a special account, Captain Maclain."

"And you get a commission on everything a client of yours sells whether or not it's sold by you?"

"Yes," said Sarah Hanley, "that's true."

"Ten per cent, isn't it?"

"Yes."

"If the client sells something himself, he's supposed to remit the commission to you?"

"Yes." Sarah Hanley drank her cocktail and touched her lips with a tiny handkerchief.

"When a client of yours writes a book, Mrs. Hanley, tell me just what you do."

"I read it first, of course." Her pleasant answers hid a certain amount of antagonism. "If I don't think it's perfect, I suggest revisions. If I like it, I send one copy to a publisher, and another copy to one of the magazines where I think the book might have a serial sale."

The Captain said, "There are other rights, too?"

"Of course. The author has a chance for movie rights, reprints in the cheap editions, and foreign sale."

The Captain took his lighter from his pocket, twirled it in his fingers, and replaced it. "Do you tell your clients where you're submitting their work?"

"No. That's especially true when they're new. Established ones have regular publishers, and most of the time regular magazine markets. If I tried to keep all of them informed what I was doing all the time, I'd never be able to make a sale." She leaned forward, drumming her fingers on a leather-topped desk. "My books are audited regularly, Captain Maclain. I remit money to my clients within twenty-four hours after I have it in my hands."

The Captain said gently, "I'm sure you do, Mrs. Hanley. What I'm getting at is the fact that if it becomes necessary to check up on Larmar's income for the past year, the easiest way to do it would be through you."

Sarah Hanley leaned back mollified. "Yes, that's quite true. Everything that Larmar makes through his writing passes through my office."

The telephone rang. Sarah Hanley picked it up and said, "Captain, it's for you."

The room was silent as he took the phone, said "Hello," and listened without speaking, gently fingering the side of his jaw. "I'll come over," he said at last, and hung up.

"Sybella?" asked Lucia.

"She was conscious for a while," said Duncan Maclain. His rugged face was furrowed as though he might be trying to part some mental curtain. "That was the police," he said at last.

"Did she say anything?" asked Paul.

The Captain turned his sightless eyes toward the other side of the room. "She talked a little. She found some clippings in Troy's apartment, and a profile of Daniel Pine."

"Clippings?" repeated Sarah Hanley.

"Some of them had had pink paper pasted on the back." The Captain swung toward his hostess. "Pink paper, Mrs. Hanley. May I have my hat? That knowledge is frightfully dangerous for her. It means she mustn't be left alone."

2

Hospitals and prisons bore a disagreeable kinship to each other in the mind of Duncan Maclain. They had the same corridors, the same cushioned footsteps, the same disturbing smell of enforced sanitation. Their cubicles stretched out in tiers, all of them monotonously housing pain. All the inmates were unwilling visitors, anxious to leave and never return. After all, the doctors and interns were only more kindly wardens whose uniforms were invisible to Duncan Maclain.

Davis and Detective Riker met him in the lobby at the East River hospital.

Davis said, "Riker has the notes he made when Sybella talked."

The doctor came up.

Maclain asked, "How is she?"

The doctor took his arm. "You can go in if you want to, but I'm afraid she's lapsed again."

They started down the corridor together, with Davis and Riker following. The hall felt cool and the wall was smooth to the Captain's fingers. Schnucke eased him gently to one side giving passage to a rubber-tired stretcher wheeled by a soft-shod orderly.

"How long does this sort of thing go on?" asked Maclain.

The doctor's hand closed reassuringly on the Captain's arm. "You're giving yourself a lot of needless worry. Now that she's come around I'm practically certain she'll be all right. Patients often regain consciousness and lose it again. She's had a fairly serious injury to the brain."

A nurse went by and gazed in starched disapproval at Schnucke.

The Captain asked, "Have you any idea when she might recover again?"

"None," said the doctor. "It's always uncertain when—"

"You said that before," the Captain reminded him bitterly. "When patients have a fairly serious injury to the brain."

The doctor said, "You're upsetting yourself needlessly, Captain Maclain."

They went in the room and the Captain sat down on a metal chair beside the bed. His fingers crept over the table top, touched the bulb in the bed light and pulled away. He pictured Davis and Riker standing on the other side of the high narrow bed and the doctor at the foot. The doctor was talking about orientation and saying,

"You can't always believe what patients say when they first recover consciousness. They're not always oriented when they've had an injury to the brain. I had a patient not so long ago whose car was struck by a fire truck. She remembered it instantly when she recovered, but she thought there had been three trucks instead of one. Her story was accurate enough, except for the three."

The Captain was listening to Sybella's breathing. "She has a fever," he remarked.

"A little," the doctor admitted, glancing at Maclain, "but it's nothing serious."

"Nothing in life is serious," said Duncan Maclain.

"I don't believe I understand," said the doctor.

"That's because you're not blind," the Captain told him. "You're a good doctor so you have to stay detached from suffering. If a case becomes too serious to you, it warps your judgment. But I can't see it, so I have to feel it with my brain."

Davis sat down in the small wooden armchair.

The doctor stood resting his hands on the foot of the bed, still looking puzzled.

"Can we believe anything of what she's already said?" asked Maclain, and added with smooth irony, "Always taking into consideration her fairly serious injury to the brain."

"Certainly," said the doctor. "It's quite possible that she was oriented although—"

"There's always an element of doubt." The Captain nodded.

"Yes, an element of doubt." The doctor raised his sleeve to look at his watch. "If you need me, I'll be in the hospital."

"Thank you," said Maclain.

The doctor went out, and closed the door carefully behind him.

"I should think they could oil their hinges, Davis."

The inspector twisted around in his chair and looked at the door. "I didn't hear anything."

"It would drive me crazy," the Captain said, "if I was lying ill in here."

Detective Riker shuffled his feet on the other side of the bed.

Davis asked, "Do you want to hear what she said? Riker has the notes."

"Yes."

The detective took a leather-bound book from his pocket, leafed over pages and began to read. "I was stationed at the bedside of Sybella Ford in room forty-three of the East River—"

"You're not on the witness stand. Let's hear what she had to say," said Duncan Maclain.

Riker turned a page. "'I was very careless. Will you tell Captain Maclain? Somebody was back of the curtain and hit me. I tried to scream, but they hit me again. There were clippings in the drawer. Felix Nightingale. A widow named Cornelia Brown. There was a man found beaten by a railroad siding and something about a suicide, and lots of others. It's hard to remember. There was a necktie, a blue one, in Troy's closet. The *New Yorkers* in the drawer with the clippings had a profile of Daniel Pine. Duncan wanted to know—what she kept—'"

"Her eyes are open," said Davis.

"Feeling better, darling?" asked Maclain. He found her hand and closed his fingers about it.

"Yes, better," Sybella said.

Davis left his chair and moved closer. "You look very pretty in the white turban."

"I have a headache," Sybella said softly, "but I'm not in any great pain. Can I have some water?"

Davis put the glass tube to her lips and she sipped a few times without moving. He took the water away.

Sybella said, "How are you, Duncan?"

"Fine," said Maclain.

"I botched things up," said Sybella.

"I'm the one who's botched them up," said Duncan Maclain.

"There were clippings in the drawer."

She spoke so low that the Captain bent closer to hear her. He said, "We know all that, darling. Now go to sleep again."

"The tie came from Hylkers."

Riker wrote it down.

"Go to sleep now," said Maclain.

"Felix Nightingale and the widow named Brown and her second son were killed by a taxi and lots of the clippings had pink paper pasted to the back as though something had been torn away."

"We know about the paper, darling. Now go to sleep."

He leaned over and gently kissed her, and after a while she smiled and said, "That was worth getting hit on the head for, Captain Duncan Maclain."

Detective Riker snapped a rubber band around his notebook. "She's gone to sleep again."

"Stick close to her, Riker, until you're relieved," Davis ordered and added, "Are you coming, Maclain?"

They left the bedroom together, and out on First Avenue Davis said, "I want coffee."

"With a side dish of information?" the Captain asked.

"Put it anyway you like. There's a diner a block farther down."

The drizzle had turned to a fine Scotch mist.

The Captain walked tranquilly along holding to Davis's arm, and offering nothing.

They had gone half a block when Davis said, "What are you cooking? You're too damn calm."

"There are times, Larry," said Duncan Maclain, "when I view myself with alarm."

"Now what's the trouble?"

"My brain keeps splitting itself," said Maclain. "You look at a person, and listen. I can't look at anybody so I listen and think of something else. I've been thinking of the word *darling*, Larry. I've only used it to one person in my entire life and that's Sybella. Yet today, it's a term of endearment which has ceased being a term of endearment because so many people throw it promiscuously around."

"If this has anything to do with the stabbing of that man this afternoon in your penthouse," said Davis, "maybe I'd better put in for a spot in the retired policemen's farm."

"I think if we both moved up there," said Duncan Maclain, "it wouldn't do any harm."

They entered the lunchwagon and found a booth by one of the windows. The Captain went on without interruption as soon as they sat down.

"Would one woman call another one darling, Larry, if she'd never seen the woman before?"

"Who the hell knows what women will do?" asked Davis. "Who did?"

The Captain said, "Her name was Troy."

"And who's her darling?" asked Davis.

"Sarah Hanley," said Duncan Maclain. "Troy came into Larmar's cocktail party while Sarah Hanley was sitting beside me. She said, 'Hello, darling', and just a little later I heard her tell Larmar out on the terrace that she knew nobody there. I think it might pay you, Davis, to find out what the reticent Mrs. Hanley really does know about Troy."

Down First Avenue, a hook and ladder swung in from a cross street and started on a run uptown. As it passed the diner, its whistle shrieked loose a warning with a frightful staccato din. Under the table, Schnucke pressed closer to the Captain's leg and began to tremble.

A waiter put coffee down.

The Captain said, "You see, Larry, that split mind of mine has been working again. Brownie Mitchell was going to hold an experiment for me in his gun shop tonight and now he doesn't need to." The Captain slowly stirred his coffee and sipped it. "I think you'd better work along with me, Larry, and quit being so damned stubborn. I just found out this minute who murdered Troy."

3

The Captain found Sergeant Archer waiting for him at the penthouse. Most of the wreckage attendant upon Gallagher's murder had been cleared away.

Archer, a normally silent man except for occasional wisecracks in keeping with his heavy sense of humor, was in a talkative mood. He followed Maclain into the office, watched him dispose of his raincoat and remove Schnucke's guiding brace, and said, "This has been a lovely day."

The Captain smiled. "I gather from the direction of your voice that you're staring toward the liquor cabinet. Fix yourself a drink."

"You too?"

"No." Maclain took his place behind his desk and lit a cigarette, listening to the sergeant busy at the bar.

When Archer was settled in a chair, the Captain called Brownie Mitchell on the telephone.

"You needn't waste any more time on experiments, Brownie. I know how that gun was fired. —No, it wasn't by radio. —No, I'll show you tomorrow afternoon in Larmar's apartment. Five o'clock. That'll give us time to set things up. Good-by." He cradled the phone and took his jigsaw puzzle from the drawer.

Archer swallowed noisily and said, "How?"

The Captain dumped the fifty-piece puzzle out on his desk. "I'm not going to say."

"I don't believe you know," said Archer. "You're not one to keep things from the police when you're sure."

"You wouldn't believe me if I told you." The Captain's fingers went to work among the pieces, turning them paper side up, until they lay along the desk in an orderly array.

"We've learned to believe in facts, Captain," said Archer. His heavy teeth clicked as he bit the end from a cigar.

The Captain raised his head and managed to look exquisitely disgusted. "A man with a knife in his stomach is a fact, Archer. Your men are still busy clearing the evidence away."

"So Jordan didn't kill him," the sergeant stated calmly. He put a match to his cigar. "That means that he didn't kill that girl who was blackmailing him or throwing him over, or something. Isn't that what you're trying to say?"

"I'm merely intimating that there might be some connection," the Captain offered mildly. "How does one get a man out of jail, Sergeant, once you fellows have him in?"

"You prove him innocent," said Archer.

Maclain nodded agreement and found two pieces of the jigsaw puzzle which fit. "But you don't believe he's innocent, Archer."

"No."

"Will you believe it when I show you how that gun was fired tomorrow afternoon?"

"Not necessarily." The sergeant puffed stolidly. "You still won't have proved anything. The chances are a hundred to one that Jordan killed her, even though that gun could have been fired in some trick manner, which I doubt."

"It seems rather hopeless, doesn't it?" The Captain found a

third piece of the puzzle and patted it down into place. "Larmar killed Troy."

"I hope to tell you," Archer muttered.

The Captain said with irritation, "For the love of heaven, quit flicking ashes on my carpet and get yourself an ash tray."

Archer wearily moved his bulk and seated himself again.

"Larmar killed Troy," the Captain repeated, "but her hot-headed husband, the late Mr. Gallagher, arrived in New York on the previous day."

"Sure," said Archer, "let's hang it on him. He found she was running around with this writer, so he sneaked into the writer's apartment and wrote her a letter on the writer's typewriter to come up there. Then he examined all the writer's guns and found a good one. After he found the gun, he invented a gadget. He sneaked out on the terrace without anybody seeing him, and set it up. He knew his wife was going to be there on Thursday after-noon at half past five by the meeting house clock."

The Captain said, "I didn't know you were poetical, Sergeant. You've been reading *The Wonderful One-Hoss Shay.*"

"I've also read *Alice Through the Looking Glass,*" said Archer.

"You know," said Duncan Maclain, fitting another piece to his puzzle, "you help me a lot when you ramble along like that. I don't recall ever having said anything about Martin Gallagher killing his wife, but I do maintain, Archer, that somebody did almost all of the things you enumerated just now. Silly, isn't it?"

"And how!" the sergeant agreed. "How did this killer know that Troy—?"

"He didn't," Maclain said sharply. "I've been trying to point out to everybody concerned since Friday that nobody wanted to kill Troy. The gun that killed her was set for Larmar Jordan.

It was simple, but silly, and like most silly things it went wrong. A man who intends to kill a girl, Archer, doesn't fix cocktails and carry them out on a tray." The Captain held a piece of the puzzle and pointed it at his listener. "The silliness of this whole business is an element that you and Davis absolutely refuse to consider."

"It wasn't silly before you stepped in," the sergeant protested.

"It was silly before anybody stepped in," said Duncan Maclain. "A gun trap of any kind is infantile, childish, foolish and damnably uncertain, just as this one proved to be. The intended victim moved out of the way."

He paused to fit another piece. "What's even sillier, Archer, is the fact that the killer was sitting pretty until Gallagher was stabbed this afternoon. He'd killed two birds with one stone, and the help of the Homicide Squad."

"Maybe you should have us arrested," said Archer.

"Troy had been shot," the Captain continued, undisturbed, "and Larmar, the original victim, was headed for the electric chair."

"It doesn't sound very infantile to me."

"Of course it's infantile." The Captain emphasized his point by pressing down a piece of the puzzle with his thumb. "The attempt to murder Larmar was emotional, unpremeditated and unplanned."

"Now, wait a minute." Archer choked and coughed. "You've just gotten through making a stump speech about a gun trap. You say you'll show us tomorrow how that gun was discharged by chimes or what have you. What the hell's emotional about that, I want to know?"

"The planning," said Maclain. "A plan which misfires and kills somebody else isn't a plan at all. It's just plain silly *per se.*"

He threw up his head and frowned at Archer. "We're up against a killer who doesn't plan *anything,* Sergeant. That's why nothing makes sense. We're up against a killer who has all the instability of a thwarted woman. A wielder of knives, and blackjacks, and a setter of gun traps. That's the type of a killer who picks up rocks and goes for a victim in a fit of anger."

"You know something you're not telling," said Archer. He drew out a large white handkerchief and mopped his steaming brow.

"If I knew anything on God's sweet earth that would get Larmar Jordan out of jail and that you and Davis would believe, I'd have told you long before now." The Captain's cigarette had burned to nothing in the tray beside him, and the puzzle was a third completed. "You've the resources I lack, Archer. You've men to make inquiries, and laboratories, and operators who can search an apartment. I've tried to mix in, and Sybella tried to help me. She's in the hospital right now."

"What do you want us to do, Maclain?" The Sergeant's voice was gruff.

"They're some things I can't see," said Duncan Maclain. "I want a description of the kind of neckties worn by every man remotely connected with the Jordans and Troy. I particularly want to know what men are addicted to cheap neckties, and bows. Sybella found a tie that came from Hylkers in Troy's apartment. Ties start there at five dollars and up. The man she bought it for didn't like it, so he left it at her place. Possibly as a concession, he'd wear it when he went out with Troy. You might check Hylkers and see if they remember the purchase. It's a long slim chance, but she might have had an account there, and they'd know whom she bought it for." Maclain leaned forward, his long, strong hands poised on the desk like spiders ready to jump.

"We've worked together for a long time, Archer, and most of all I want you to believe me."

"Maybe I do," said Archer, "but I'm a member of the Homicide Squad. What else are you looking for?"

"I'm looking for a clipping bureau that attaches pink slips to their clippings. If you find it, I want to know if they had an account for Troy." He leaned back. "I wish this wasn't Sunday."

"Why?"

"Because an emotional, unstable criminal strikes any place without warning," said Duncan Maclain. "Such a criminal is always ready. He sets a gun trap, and waits. But he always has a knife or a blackjack when he needs it. The trouble is, Archer, he doesn't know himself when he'll need it. Shakespeare said, 'If it be not now, yet it will come: the readiness is all.'"

4

The sergeant left. Maclain escorted him through the anteroom, where he closed and tried the penthouse door. He returned to his desk by way of Rena's office.

When he sat down, he was holding a cylinder numbered in Braille. He fondled it for a few minutes, turning it over and over in his fingers, before he pulled the Ediphone up closer and slipped the record on. The touch of a switch connected the Ediphone with the Capehart across the room.

Maclain leaned back, wrapped in concentration as the cylinder began to play. It repeated Lucia's hysterical story, caught in full by the sensitive Detecto-Dictograph set in the wall. It went on unemotionally through the Captain's question, "*So they're holding him for murder?*" Just as impersonally, it switched from Lucia to Sybella, and back again to the voice of Paul.

With mechanical accuracy it reproduced the ringing of the telephone, the arrival of Jess Ferguson and the lawyer's statement, *"Come now, Captain, nothing's quite that hopeless. —I've just come from talking to Larmar. He's told me the truth—to that I'm ready to swear. —Let's take the bad facts."*

The Captain shut off the machine and moved nearer his desk to toy with his puzzle again.

He had taken the bad facts and considered them carefully, but Sybella's injury had let his emotions creep in and build some of the facts up out of proportion to the others. What had he told the doctor at the hospital? "You're a good doctor so you have to stay detached from suffering. If a case becomes too serious to you, it warps your judgment. But I can't see it, so I have to feel it with my brain."

He selected a piece of the puzzle and viciously fitted it in. He hadn't been using his brain at all. He'd been letting anger, affection, friendship and sympathy consume him. He'd started an analysis of the bad facts which presented themselves after the murder of Troy. What he needed to consider were the bad facts present before the murder. That was the place to begin.

This wasn't any killing for money. This was a killing as immutable as death itself. A killing fixed and foreordained through the breaking of human law. This was a problem, complex because it was simple. He'd forgotten that two right-angled triangles placed together can make a square.

The elements had all existed and he had stupidly ignored them, yet less than fifteen minutes before he had given the sergeant the answer when he'd told him, "The readiness is all."

Hatred between a man and his wife—hell hath no fury—sympathy for the lonely woman—cliches all, and old as the profession of Troy. Certainly all the elements were ready, and Duncan Maclain, dulling his brain with narcotic anger, had overlooked them all.

The puzzle was nearly completed. He swept the pieces into a drawer, and pushed his time signal button.

The operator's voice assured him it was twenty minutes to ten.

The Captain found his hat, checked his automatic, and called to Schnucke. Five minutes later he was in a cab headed downtown to have a talk with Paul Hirst.

The secretary admitted him, without surprise.

Maclain touched the sleeve of the dressing gown Paul was wearing and said, "I hope I didn't disturb you."

"I'm here alone." Paul led the way to the living room. "I turned in early to read, that's all. What did you find at the hospital?"

"Nothing much more than I told you at Sarah Hanley's." Maclain took the seat he had occupied at the cocktail party on Wednesday. "Does Larmar subscribe to a clipping bureau?"

"Yes," said Paul.

"What color are the slips they attach to their clippings?"

"It's probably Romeike's Clipping Bureau," said Paul, "if you're referring to the slips that were torn from the clippings Sybella found."

"You're smart," said Maclain.

"Clipping bureaus and writing is part of my business."

"Did Larmar ever do any newspaper stories that you know of?" Maclain relaxed against the cushions.

"Not that I know of."

"What kind of ties does Larmar wear? Bow or four-in-hand?"

"Four-in-hand, but you're mistaken if you think he ever left one up at Troy's place," said Paul.

"What makes you say that? Did anyone mention finding a tie in Troy's place?"

"Then what are you asking about them for?" Paul lit a cigarette. "He's a careful man, Captain Maclain. If he had any affairs, he kept them clear of his married life."

"You don't think he ever lived with Troy?"

"I know he didn't," said Paul.

"But I understand he ran around with women?"

"He did nearly everything to win back Lucia."

"From whom?" The Captain turned his head as though he might be looking out on the darkness of the terrace.

"Morse," said Paul.

Maclain locked his fingers around one knee. "How well did Troy Singleton know him?"

"Morse? I didn't know she knew him."

"I overheard Larmar say she knew him when she came here during the cocktail party."

"That's one on me." A switch clicked as Paul turned on a table light beside him. "Troy got around. I just found out this morning that Sarah Hanley knew her, too."

"Who told you that?"

"Gallagher," said Paul. "He called me up, wanting to come up here. I called Bob Morse because I wanted someone here during the interview."

"You said nothing about that at Sarah Hanley's this afternoon. Why not?"

"I've learned to keep my mouth shut unless people ask me questions. Besides, I wanted to see if Hanley would mention it herself. She didn't even crack when she heard about Gallagher being killed, yet he told us here this morning that he was going to talk to her."

"Did you intend to tell anybody about that fact?" asked Duncan Maclain.

"That's her business, and it's certainly not mine to involve innocent people. Morse knew about it. Let him say something if he wants to."

"Maybe you're right." The Captain unlaced his fingers. "You live here, don't you?"

"Yes."

"I tried to get some information from Larmar this afternoon." The Captain rumpled his crisp dark hair. "His memory's hazy. Maybe you can help me, Paul."

"I'll do what I can." Paul snuffed out his cigarette.

"Larmar said that on Wednesday night Brownie Mitchell was here."

"That's right."

"On Thursday morning, the day Troy was killed, Larmar went up to Sarah Hanley's, then came home, and had lunch with Bob Morse."

"Check," said Paul.

"Was Morse here at any other time that you know of within twenty-four hours before the murder?"

"No," said Paul.

The Captain stood up. "Is there a clock on the wall?"

"Yes. It's twenty past ten."

"Get me one of Larmar's pistols, will you?"

"Which one?"

"Any one, Paul. Preferably that Stotzer target pistol, if you can find it. It's similar to the gun that killed Troy."

Paul was back in a minute with the gun.

The Captain said, "I'm going to set this up on the terrace wall. You keep your eye on that clock."

He vanished into the dark dampness outside and was gone some time. When he came back in, he headed for the lavatory and flung over his shoulder, "How long did it take me?"

"About twelve minutes," said Paul.

The Captain came back in and sat down. "Whoever set that gun up out there had to take much longer than that to do it. It had to be chosen with care and sneaked out of Larmar's gun room. It had to be done when Larmar wasn't around." The Captain lowered his voice as though he might be talking to himself. "It certainly couldn't have been planted there during the cocktail party. Would Morse have had a chance to do that during lunch time?"

"He didn't go out onto the terrace during lunch time. He was with me and Larmar getting dope on the profile from the time he arrived till the time he left."

Maclain stood up frowning. "There are just too many things that don't fit in," he announced, his blind eyes fixed on Paul. "I don't believe in too many coincidences. I'm beginning to think that whoever hit Sybella knew she was going to Troy's apartment. Now I can't figure out how that gun got placed on the terrace, even though I know who fired the shot at Troy."

Paul left his seat and walked up closer to the Captain. "If you know who fired the shot at Troy, why don't you have him arrested?"

"He's already incarcerated." The Captain smiled. "He's in a cell at the veterinary's. Winnie, the cocker spaniel, fired the shot at Troy."

CHAPTER EIGHT

"The bell invites me."

I

OUTSIDE of the Jordan apartment, the Captain stopped ten paces down the hall. Schnucke looked up inquiringly. A radio was playing softly, and from a neighboring apartment the sound of a party drifted out faintly.

He turned and went back, and rang the doorbell.

Paul answered and asked, "Forget something?"

"Yes." The Captain stepped inside. "I forgot that it wouldn't make any difference when that gun was set in the terrace wall."

"I don't get it."

"You and Mitchell were cataloguing the guns, weren't you?"

"Yes."

"Do you remember the last time you came across that Buchel pistol?"

"It wasn't really part of the collection. It was a target pistol Larmar used. I don't believe we catalogued it. I still don't get what you're driving at."

"I'm driving at the fact that that Buchel pistol might have been set in place two hours, or two days, or a week before it killed Troy, so long as it was left uncocked and Larmar didn't miss it. It would have been there then, ready and waiting for the murderer to cock it by setting the hair trigger. That wouldn't take five seconds." The Captain lowered his voice and murmured, " 'The readiness is all.' "

Paul said, "She was killed by someone who knew that Winnie was scared of those church chimes and that he ran through that

188

small opening in the bushes and back of Larmar's desk and hid there every time they rang. Pretty damned clever."

The Captain nodded. "Let's go into the gun room and take a look at the catalogue.

He followed Paul.

They sat at the table and the secretary rustled leaves. "Neither the Stotzer nor the Buchel are listed in here. As I told you, they aren't really a part of the collection."

"Is a Japanese dirk with the name Osaki stamped on the back of the hilt listed there?" The Captain's hands were still on the edge of the table.

"Yes. What about it?"

"I'd like to examine it."

The Captain waited while Paul slid back his chair. A cabinet door creaked. A dagger clunked softly on the table in front of Maclain. He reached out and gingerly picked it up as Paul resumed his chair.

The Captain's sensitive fingers caressed the guard and made a journey over the ivory hilt. Light played on his face, altering it slowly from one expression to another.

"Where did you find it?" he finally asked.

Paul turned and pointed, forgetting that Maclain was blind. "It was in its usual place right there."

"Show me, please." Maclain got up.

Paul led him to a cabinet and placed Maclain's hand on the dagger's empty bed.

With agile precision, the Captain's fingers moved away to scan other weapons in the cabinet, making a detailed audit of their shape and present position.

Paul asked, "Is anything missing?"

"The reverse," said Maclain. "That dagger you just put on the table shouldn't be here. Unless I'm mistaken, it should be down at police headquarters. I felt it the other night when I was in here. Of course, the sense of touch is far from being infallible, but I think that was the dagger that was plunged into Gallagher's stomach today. I'd better make sure, although I'm certain it was in the same spot in that cabinet the last time I felt it."

He started a tour of the gun room, taking his time, using methodical care to check the weapons along the wall. With his hand on the breech of a flintlock rifle, he quit abruptly and said, "Do something, Paul. Put in a call to Long Island and get Daniel Pine. Call me when you get him. I want to check some more."

He stood where he was until Paul went into the living room, then sat down at the table. When Paul called him, he was still sitting there, twisting the hilt of the dagger around in one hand. He put it down quickly and went out to talk to Pine.

"Did you buy anything else beside that Harpers Ferry pistol from Troy Singleton?" the Captain asked without preamble, and added sharply, "You're dealing with a murder, Mr. Pine."

"You're dealing with something that's none of your business," said Pine.

"The police know that Troy sold you that pistol."

"I don't give a hoot in hell what they know," said Pine. "My collection's handled for me by accredited agents. I pay for everything I get, and it's mine."

"You paid a lot too much for that Harpers Ferry pistol," said Duncan Maclain.

"What do you mean by that crack?"

"I mean you got stuck." The Captain gave a crafty grin. "You could have probably bought it for half the price if you'd dealt through one of your accredited agents. You paid a fat price for the beauty of the seller, Mr. Pine."

"What the hell do you know about weapons?"

"You might be surprised. I can tell you where you can get some nice ones cheap."

"Such as what?"

The Captain reeled off a description of six of the pieces he had just examined in Larmar's collection. He closed by saying, "Would those appeal to you?"

"Not at any price."

"Would you mind telling me why?"

"I already have them," said Pine.

The Captain said, "I'm sorry I bothered you. I seem to have wasted your time and mine," and rang off quickly.

Paul gave a low whistle. "What was the idea of mentioning that Osaki dagger?"

"I was interested in hearing what he'd have to say, Paul. There was one of those daggers in Pine's collection."

He touched his Braille watch. "It's a little past eleven. The *Globe-Tribune's* a morning paper. Call their office for me, will you, and see if Bob Morse is there?"

Paul took the phone, and after a moment got the city desk.

"Morse is out." He covered the mouthpiece with his hand. "Will anyone else do?"

"Ask them when he'll be in?"

Paul asked and said, "He won't be in again tonight. He leaves Sunday nights at nine."

"You can hang up," the Captain told him. "I found out what I want to know. I'm going down there. That's perfectly fine."

You notice things that others miss when you live in a world of sound. Equally, you might miss things that others notice. Those were axioms which Duncan Maclain had found.

The door that closed behind you.

Music from a radio.

Untroubled laughter.

You were walking in the footsteps of a man who had lived that morning. He had closed that same door behind him, trod that same carpet. His thumb had rested where your thumb was, pushing the elevator button marked "Down."

What had he heard? Had the radio been playing in the morning? Had he heard the same laughter of happy people? Had he heard the bell ring fourteen floors below as Maclain could hear it?

Maybe he'd never gone to see Sarah Hanley. Maybe, as you did, waiting in the hallway, he'd heard another sound. Well, dead men give no answers, but that man had eyes; the sharp, trained eyes of an ex-policeman. Maybe he'd also heard and seen footfalls, made light as a woman's by caution. Maybe he'd caught a single glimpse of a head thrust out of a service door. A blind man could hear, but he couldn't see. He could only know that a door had closed far down the hall.

Had the dead man ever read Shakespeare? Had he ever muttered, "The readiness is all"? Or had he become the stalker, and followed the stealthy footsteps himself because he knew who owned them. That might easily be the answer. That might be why he'd never paid Hanley a call.

Or perhaps he'd pushed the button again and heard it ring far below him. He could have told by looking whether or not he stood alone in the hall. The blind only knew by listening and thinking.

It was doubtful that the dead man feared imagination. Imagination was foaled in darkness. It was doubtful that he'd read *Macbeth* or *Hamlet*. It was doubtful that hearing the bell ring far below him he had thought it might be like the carillon, no more than a death knell.

> "The bell invites me.
>   Hear it not, Duncan; for it is a knell
>   That summons thee to heaven
>   Or to hell."

It was very doubtful that the dead man knew enough Shakespeare to have ever heard that "The readiness is all."

2

Hot or cold, sleet or snow, sunshine or storm, the weather was only a matter of sensation to Duncan Maclain. If he felt elated basking in the sun, it had nothing to do with visual brightness. Rather it was due to a high pressure area or the pleasing warmth of a sun-basked skin.

Rain might depress him, not because the night was darker or the skies were gray, but because he was keenly conscious of its monotonous patter and dampened objects were naturally disagreeable to touch and feel. There was also the added factor that the spirits of the world dropped when the barometer was low.

Through years of blindness, the Captain had set up a bodily defense against the dejection of dampness. He might be sprightly and gay and expansive when the world about him scintillated with dancing sunshine. He protected himself from melancholy, always dangerous to a blind man, by shutting it out with an armor of mental steel.

Still, there was something stimulating about dampness to Duncan Maclain. It heightened the sound-carrying properties of the atmosphere, and his audacity and belief in himself were enhanced in direct proportion to his ability to hear. Sounds which he might have missed became audible and definable when the myriad noises of civilization were stilled by a blanket of mist and rain. Playing with death, the sensitivity of his ears as well as his fingers meant life to Duncan Maclain.

Just a few hours before, murder had followed in the train of a set of footsteps. The Captain knew he was overwrought and that the footsteps might have been present only in the eye of fancy, but leaving the Arday Apartments he felt convinced that he had heard them again. The footsteps had been clever during the afternoon, devilishly clever. The Captain decided not to underrate them.

The doorman had left for the night, but the elevator boy asked, "Can I get a taxi, sir?"

"Thank you, I'll walk."

Escorted by Schnucke, he struck off up Fifth Avenue, tucking himself deeper into his light waterproof coat against the feel of the misty rain.

Schnucke checked him at the first crossing. A couple was talking half a block ahead. Two automobiles stopped to await the change of traffic lights.

Schnucke took him forward, crossing Eleventh Street. The brief pause had been enough to tell him that so far there was no one behind him. A halt was equivalent to a look over the shoulder in the progress of Duncan Maclain.

A block farther on, several people came out of Longchamps restaurant. They were talking animatedly as they passed in front of the Captain. Filtered through the distracting sounds of the conversation, he thought he heard the footsteps again. The people got in a taxi and slammed the door. The cab rolled off, and Maclain stood quite still.

A second cab pulled up to discharge a single passenger. Change tinkled. A man passed by, and there was a noise as the driver raised his flag.

A voice said, "Taxi, mister? I don't mind your dog."

The Captain said, *"Globe-Tribune* building," and got in.

The Cab made a U-turn, heading downtown. At Eighth Street it slowed, and two other cars went by.

Maclain sat back in the seat, absently caressing Schnucke's damp coat.

The cab turned east to Broadway where it headed south. The street was deserted with a Sunday night deadness.. The man at the wheel drove swiftly and no other cars went by.

The dampness seemed heavier when they stopped downtown.

The driver hopped out and opened the door. "Can I see you inside, Mister? This is the *Globe-Tribune.*"

"To the elevator, if you don't mind." Maclain put a hand on the driver's arm. Inside, he gave him a bill and said, "Keep the change."

An elevator man asked, "Where to?"

"I want to talk to the night city editor." Maclain heard the taxi driver whisper, "That guy's blind."

A woman came in and entered the car accompanied by a swish of skirts and a smell of perfume.

The car shot up. The woman got out at the eleventh floor. The car went higher, and the operator said, "You get off here, Mister. This is twenty, the city room."

Maclain stepped out, and the door slid shut behind him. A boy took him in charge and conducted him for eighty paces across a noisy room. A wooden chair was by a desk. The Captain touched it and sat down.

An interested voice said, "I'm McVeigh. Couldn't I have

helped you by phone? This is a hell of a night to haul all the way downtown."

"I'm interested in a couple of news stories," said Maclain. "The only information I have about them is that one concerns a fellow named Felix Nightingale and the other one's about a widow named Cornelia Brown. There're some others, but my information is too indefinite to identify them."

"Your information still isn't very definite on the first two." The man at the desk laughed shortly, and sucked at a noisy pipe. "What happened to this Nightingale and Brown?"

"All I know is that the widow had a second son who was killed by a taxi. I don't know anything about Felix Nightingale except that something was written about him. There're some other stories, but I've no names. One concerned a man beaten near a railroad siding."

"Wait a minute," said McVeigh. "I know who covers that sort of thing. I'll get his file."

A pencil scribbled on a pad. A boy came up. Near by, a typewriter clattered briefly. The boy went away and McVeigh talked over a telephone. After a while the boy came back.

McVeigh was silent a moment before he said, "Felix Nightingale was a sergeant in the Army who came to New York to get married and lost his girl in the crowd. Human interest stuff. You want the details?"

"Not necessarily. I'm interested more in the stories than the details."

"The Brown woman had a son in the Army who was killed in action, and the day she got the message she had another son run over by a taxicab. She wasn't exactly a widow. Her husband was in the penitentiary in Arkansas. More human interest stuff."

"Who wrote them?" asked the Captain.

"Bob Morse covers all that sort of thing." McVeigh chuckled. "It isn't really news. We run them more on account of his sob sister style. Now here's the one about the man who was beaten up near the railroad siding. A fellow named Fitzgerald." He read it, and more.

The Captain listened politely, and then asked, "How long ago were those written?"

"Quite a few months ago," said McVeigh, "but there have been more recent ones. Do you want to see them?"

The Captain said, "No. Thanks very much. As a matter of fact, it was the style I was interested in." He gave a sheepish grin. "There's been some talk of Bob Morse putting me into a profile."

"You're famous enough around here to make a good one, Captain Maclain. If Morse wants time off to do it, have him tell me."

"He's off tonight, isn't he?"

"Yes." The editor's voice carried irritation. "He's a damned good writer, but he has a fault. He likes his liquor."

The Captain said, "Don't we all?" and stood up.

On the way to the elevator, he asked McVeigh, "Where does Morse live?"

"He has an apartment on East Tenth Street." McVeigh gave the number. "I've been up there a couple of times. It's a two flight walk-up, third floor front. He's a late riser though. If you want to catch him, just lean on the third bell button till he finally lets you in."

3

Maclain went down and caught another cab.

His eyes were narrowed with undue strain as he gave Bob Morse's address and quickly clambered in.

The picture was taking terrible shape, coming into startling focus to present a killer who had no scruples, a killer with experience, who had struck before and would readily strike again. It had shaped so fast that Duncan Maclain knew he must act just as swiftly. For the first time in his life, he had so much at stake that he dared not fail. The trouble was that with all his skill, he didn't know where to begin.

He sat all through the ride uptown with his forehead deep in furrows. Schnucke, who sensed his every mood, kept pressed close to him.

When the cab rolled off and left him on the silent stretch of East Tenth Street, he walked up the steps with a caution so great that it caused an unpleasant tingling under his skin. With his finger close to the button above the third box, he stopped and pushed the first button instead. Down in the basement, a bell gave a quick sharp ring. In a few seconds' time, a buzzer answered.

The Captain opened the street door, put a foot in the crack and waited.

Outside, from a basement window, somebody called, "Why don't you push the right bell, you drunken bum?"

Off in the distance a steeple clock struck a single note. Inside the house, another echoed the chime.

The Captain opened the door, and merging with Schnucke, climbed the stairs like a disembodied shadow.

Third floor front.

He listened for five full minutes, then tried the door without a sound. It was unlocked, so he pushed it ajar for an inch or two and listened again. Satisfied at last, he opened it and went on in.

He had to know something and know it fast. If he only knew where to begin.

Schnucke led him around a chair and stopped at a desk. A whisky bottle was nearly empty. The light bulb in the desk light was cold.

The Captain toured a sitting room and bedroom and at last found book shelves stuffed with volumes. The bottom ones were stacked with magazines. His fingers flitted over the piles and stopped at the *New Yorkers,* recognizable instantly because they were thin. He riffled through the two on top, but the volumes were empty.

The third, fourth, fifth and sixth held clippings shoved in the back. There were more in the ninth and tenth. It was obvious now that Morse had a habit of using *New Yorkers* to serve as files.

The Captain stacked them up again and turned to search for the telephone. With his hand outstretched, he stopped.

He had left the apartment door open, the better to hear. Downstairs, someone entered, using a latch key. There was a murmur of voices, and a "Thank you."

Two sets of feet climbed the stairs to the second floor. One set disappeared, lost in the opening and closing of a door. The second set continued, climbing steadily.

The Captain knew that a showdown had come. He might postpone it temporarily by closing and bolting the apartment door, but now was as good a time as any. The footsteps were bent on the destruction of Duncan Maclain and Sybella Ford, who knew too much about clippings, but as long as the footsteps were near Maclain, Sybella Ford was safe.

Death was moving quietly but purposefully down the hall. The Captain backed into the bedroom, holding Schnucke close beside him, and letting it come.

The footsteps stopped in the living room while the owner

turned the desk light on, then moved still closer to the bedroom door.

Speaking out of the shadows, the Captain said, "My dog will tear you to pieces if you pull a gun. Even if you shoot before he gets you, you'll still have lost for I'm a deadly shot at sound. The best thing you can do right now is to sit down quietly."

The owner of the footsteps chuckled and came confidently on to enter the bedroom.

The Captain heard breathing, and tensing every muscle, launched himself at the sound. He crashed into an unseen stool, taking it on the shin. A fist in brass knuckles cut a three inch gash across his chin and split his lips. He went back down, slamming his head against a partly opened bureau drawer. The only lights that Maclain could see were the lights of pain that flashed out brightly as he struck the floor, and a booted foot smashed into his side, caving two ribs in.

The Captain smiled a horrible smile. He'd played a tough game for years and now, at last, a killer was going to win.

It was then he learned that even a man who has owned one for years can't always tell what a dog will do. For the only time in her gentle life, Schnucke barked a bark of real defiance, which ended in a terrifying growl. Above Maclain a voice snapped out an oath that was full of panic. A heavy vase shattered, raining pieces about Maclain, and Schnucke stopped.

The Captain reached for his gun and found that he lacked the strength to pull and fire. But Schnucke did her part almost as well as Dreist. The footsteps hurried across the sitting room, descended the stairs and were gone.

The Captain's attempt to move himself lit once more the lights of wracking pain. He knew without thinking that if the silencing blow on Schnucke had ever found him, he would never have moved again.

With pinwheels whirling inside him, he bumped into a rocking chair as he tried to crawl to the door. Something was moving near him, slithering across the floor. A wet tongue touched his bloody cheek and everything human fled out of Duncan Maclain. With his hand on the whimpering Schnucke, he got to the sitting room and touched the desk before the dog lay still.

The desk upset with a startling crash, and his hand moved slowly, searching the singing note of the dial tone as the telephone fell beside him. He found the base and dialed fast, entirely oblivious to the flaming stabs of pain.

"Get Sybella Ford out of that hospital room. Get her out! Great God, don't ask questions, get her out of there!"

"Who is this?" asked the frightened telephone girl.

"I'm the messenger of God! A murdering bastard just tried to kill my dog and me. I'm going to flay him alive before morning!" He drew a breath and choked, then sputtered out more calmly, "This is what's left of Captain Duncan Maclain."

There were few people living who knew the depth and danger hidden beneath the calm exterior of Duncan Maclain. Life itself had hurt him so badly that in beating it, he had almost lost the capacity to feel any personal pain. When twenty teeth have ached for years, it's difficult to distinguish any one.

Living just for the sake of living meant nothing to the Captain, but living as a game was crammed to the hilt with emotion. You played the game to win, of course; if you lost it, you died. So what the hell, dying itself could be a lot of fun.

It was other lives that kept him going. Spud and Rena, Cappo Marsh and Sarah, Schnucke and Dreist, Davis and Archer, and recently, Sybella Ford had become an important one. They were symbols in his fertile mind, gilded perhaps, and worshiped out of all proportion because they had no faults or foibles to a man who could not see. Hurt one of them, and you drilled a nerve in the soul of Duncan Maclain.

That was dangerous. He became a man devoid of pity, stealthy and fast and tricky as a crawling bushmaster, and as poisonous in his hunt for retribution, doubly deadly because of his icy impersonality. There was only one law—an eye for an eye—in a world where you could not see; a world of blackness, where taking chances was foolish; a world where those who loved you and protected you existed only as unseen figments of reality.

With Schnucke's heavy body trembling in his arms, he was a man gone mad, a frightful figure stumbling down a staircase onto Tenth Street. He had a plan, but it was wild and irrational as something thought up by a native run amok on an island in the Coral Sea. Bleeding and disheveled and holding his dog, he staggered out onto the roadway.

An automobile screeched to a stop, and a man said, "Jesus!"

The Captain stumbled against the side of the car and slithered through the open door.

"St. Vincent's hospital's only a block away." The driver started to turn, ignoring the one way street.

The Captain arranged Schnucke tenderly on his lap, took out a handkerchief and wiped his own smashed lips.

"I haven't got time for St. Vincent's or anything else." He coughed and shivered. "Drive uptown to the East River hospital, and for Christ's sake, hurry."

****

When you are blind, the night is still and the hours are long. A shade may flap at a window and curtains may blow. A house can creak and water can drip and trees can move and rustle their branches together, and madness comes close through sheer monotony.

They had moved Sybella an hour before. Lying rigid in the bed she'd occupied, with bandages wound tight about his shattered ribs, Maclain lay listening.

The hospital was a house of quiet. He grinned up at the ceiling, a grin that would have turned a watcher cold. A chime kept ringing, calling some doctor who never seemed to answer. The chime was supposed to be soft and soothing to the patients. It pounded into the Captain's ears with the force of a small steam hammer. Two and five and three. Then it would stop and start again, and change its number as though that made any difference.

One and three and three.

Soft-soled shoes shuffled along a padded floor. A stretcher rolled noiselessly. Somewhere a leaky toilet trickled without cessation. The room door opened and the nurse looked in.

"Asleep?"

Maclain closed his eyes and set his painful lips. The nurse departed and left him wondering how many patients had died from listening to the squeak of one of her shoes.

Far down the corridor a child roused the night with a hacking cough, and began to cry. The Captain's fingers moved under the sheet, unwinding the bandage steadily. The gong took up its stuttering call, hunting for two five three.

The bandage came off. He folded it into a three-foot length and twisted it into a strangler's cord, then stretched it out beside him and lay back gingerly.

Doctors wore masks and gowns and looked alike in their white disguise. Hospitals were unwary. A man who had killed before had nerve. His nerve would get him a mask and gown, and masked and gowned, he might walk the hall without objection. But masked and gowned, he could not hide footsteps that had shuffled along the cold hard flags of a penitentiary. He was quite close now, and the door had closed and he'd stopped inside.

The light would not help him much this time, for Maclain had unscrewed all the bulbs with a kind of awful glee.

The Captain lay and listened and his brain worked fast, speeding along with heady, happy clarity. It might be a knife or a bludgeon, or maybe simple smothering. A woman with a fractured skull was easy to kill. But the killer had to come nearer, and hand to hand with the messenger of God, there wasn't a chance in the darkness for a killer who could not see.

Three steps nearer, and Maclain had wound his strangler's bandage tight around one hand and slid down the blankets without a sound.

One step nearer, and a hand moved out to locate the head on the pillow. The Captain's fingers closed about a wrist with the calm cold strength of a devil fish. His brain flashed bright with the pain of his ribs as he twisted an arm into a paralyzing hold, whirling the masked figure. In the space of a breath, the strangler's bandage had fallen over the cursing head, and tightened.

"Funny place to come looking for that clipping about your wife and kids, Brownie," said Duncan Maclain. "Did you expect to find it with Sybella or with me?"

4

Davis and Archer were deep in the middle of an animated rehash when a nurse wheeled the bandaged and taped up Captain into the hospital superintendent's office on the following afternoon.

The Captain asked, "What's the idea of having me trundled all over the hospital? Why couldn't you come to my room?"

Davis said, "I brought a record up for you. I thought it might help heal your ribs if I played it on the Ediphone."

Archer squirmed on an office chair. "Some day we're going to have to arrest you for murder, Captain. You nearly had that guy strangled to death last night before we could get into your room."

"What did you want me to do? Kiss him?" asked Duncan Maclain. "There're times when you fellows are a little slow on the uptake."

"How the hell did I know he was a killer?" Archer demanded hotly. "He had on a doctor's mask and gown. He came walking down the hall and suddenly vanished into your room."

"What did you think he was going to wear?" Davis produced a toothpick and a scowl.

The Captain grinned maliciously. "The sergeant expects his murderers to stay true to type, Larry. They're supposed to wear black masks like Ellery Queen and walk down hospital corridors carrying a gun." He turned toward Archer and said more seriously, "You did just right to let him get in, Sergeant. That's what I wanted. You and your men kept out of sight as I asked you to. If he'd been suspicious at all he wouldn't have showed up, and you'd have spoiled all my fun."

"God deliver me from your idea of play," said Davis. "I hope nobody ever kicks Schnucke when you're walking down Fifth Avenue. And as to your detective methods—" He broke his toothpick and dropped it in a wastebasket. "You're just a plain murdering son of a gun. Some day somebody's going to get you first."

"They all think that. That's what makes life interesting," said Duncan Maclain. "What's this record?"

"There're several."

"I don't want to hear them all." The Captain held up his hands protestingly. "At least not now. Did you get any statement out of him as to what he did yesterday?"

Davis selected a record. "I've boiled the gist of it down onto one. You can listen to it and then ask questions." He clamped the earphones about the Captain's head and started the Ediphone. "*I'd known Rose Gallagher who went by the name of Troy Singleton for a long time. Her husband, Martin Gallagher, warned me to keep away from her, threatening to kill me. I'd gotten into a mess in Arkansas. Gallagher, who was on the New York force then, found it out and had me sent away.*

"*When I got out, Gallagher had gone into the Army. Troy was in the money, and I started living with her, although my wife, Cornelia Brown, is still alive.*

"*I've always known a lot about guns. Troy had gotten a lot of money out of Jordan. She got me in with him. At my suggestion she offered to get him a good price for his Harpers Ferry pistol by selling it herself to Pine. She'd known Bob Morse when she was check girl at a night club. She borrowed a couple of old New Yorkers from him because they had a lot of dope in them about Pine's guns and also about Pine.*

"*I got a bad break. Morse had covered a story when my sons were killed. He had shoved it with some clippings in the back of the* New Yorkers *with the profile of Pine. I don't know whether Troy saw it or not, and I didn't know whether Morse had put it there on purpose. I didn't dare take it out, although it worried me all the time. I was afraid that Troy would get suspicious if she'd seen it, or that Morse would miss it when the* New Yorkers *were returned, and connect it with me.*

"*When Jordan asked me to make a fake pistol for him so that one of the main pieces of his collection wouldn't be missed—he likes to put up a front—I got an idea. I started duplicating his other pieces and selling them to Pine. I'd looted most of the good things in his collection and last month I heard he was going to sell it.*

"I decided to kill him. I hadn't only looted his collection, but he was breaking me up with Troy. She thought she was in love with him. Up until the time he came in the picture, everything between us had been fine.

"I'd watched his cocker spaniel, Winnie, who was scared of the church chimes, and ran through the hedge in back of Larmar's desk whenever they rang. I'd been working on Larmar's guns since Spring. I got interested in the dog and saw that it used the same opening in the hedge every time. I made experiments in my shop.

"The wall of the terrace had slots in it. The box hedges are pressed close against the wall. I rigged the gun up three weeks ago and tested it without loading it, until I found that by wrapping a handkerchief around the butt, wedging it in one of the slots, and resting the barrel in the bushes, and crossing two twigs through the trigger guard, the dog would fire it every time. I made more experiments in my shop until I found just how to fix it so that it would kick itself out of the wall. Finally I loaded the gun, and kept it loaded for several days. Rain wouldn't bother it at all, and since Larmar only used the pistol in target matches, he wouldn't miss it. The night before Troy was killed, I slipped out when Paul was in the bathroom, and cocked the gun.

"I didn't intend to kill Troy. She just happened to be there at that time. I wrote the note and had her come up to the cocktail party. Jordan's wife was the logical one to kill him. There would be plenty of witnesses that he'd thrown Troy right in his wife's

face, if anything went wrong. I never thought the gun would kill Troy. I'd have been okay if it hadn't been for Gallagher and Maclain.

"*Saturday night Sybella Ford surprised me in Troy's apartment. I hit her and took the clippings and the New Yorkers. She also found a tie that Troy had bought for me. I destroyed the New Yorkers, the clippings and the tie, but I was afraid that Sybella Ford had read that clipping, and I hoped she'd die before she told it to Maclain.*

"*Yesterday morning I went down to talk to Paul. Martin Gallagher came out of the Jordans' apartment as I got out of the elevator. I was scared to death for I didn't even know he was in town. He always hated me and would have killed me without question if he'd found out I'd been living with Troy.*

"*Sarah Hanley was dangerous to me too, but not so much. She'd only known that Rose Gallagher had been mixed up with a married man named Brown, but she'd never seen me, and there are lots of Browns. Everybody always called me Brownie and I couldn't shake it even after I took the name of Mitchell. I decided it was safer to keep the middle name of Brown.*

"*As quick as I was, Gallagher must have seen me in the hall, although I ducked into a stairway and ran down. I waited until he came out on Fifth Avenue. I followed him to his hotel and later downtown. He tried to get in to talk to Larmar, but Maclain and his lawyer were there. I was in back of them as they came out, but I lost Gallagher. He was very slick at shaking shadows.*

"*Later in the afternoon, I realized that he'd started following me. I knew then that I'd have to kill him. I went to my shop and got a duplicate of the Osaki dagger. I'd done a good job on it. There was a fake in Larmar's collection, and I'd sold the*

*original to Pine. I thought it would confuse the police if I used
a third one.*

"Gallagher followed me to Maclain's apartment house. I
thought if I could get him alone in the stair well, I could wait
for him and kill him before he got me. I'd learned a trick in
prison about getting a man who was carrying a gun. I got him
on the twenty-fourth floor.

"When I got back to the shop, Maclain telephoned and said
he'd discovered how the Buchel pistol was fired on the terrace.
He was causing me all my trouble, throwing off the police who
had a perfect case against Jordan. Gallagher had made things
tough enough. Now I had to dispose of Maclain and Sybella
Ford before I could call it a day. I decided to get it over with
quickly.

"I picked him up at Seventy-second Street and followed him
downtown. I couldn't get him at the Jordans' or at the Globe-
Tribune building. He played into my hands at Morse's. I got a
break there because I knew Morse hadn't answered the door when
Maclain got in. Then I got a second break. A man came along.
I told him I was spending the week end with Morse and he let
me in.

"The only thing I overlooked was the police dog. He went
for me or I'd have finished Maclain. As it was, I thought I'd put
him in the hospital for a long time. If I was successful with Sybella Ford, and Maclain didn't kick in, I could try again.

"I waited until later to come up to the hospital. I knew they
might be guarding Sybella Ford's room, but I figured I could get
a mask and gown out of the supply room without arousing suspicion. I took a chance, and did it, and walked right in."

The record clicked off.

The Captain removed the earphones and said, "He was so

damn dumb he was smart, Larry. That happens sometimes. Whoever rigged that pistol had to know all about guns and had to have the opportunity." His rugged face grew thoughtful. "I'm glad that Schnucke's going to be all right. She was the one who nailed him, after all."

"Don't worry, she'll get all the credit." Davis wrapped himself in irony. "The papers don't know there's a police force in existence when there's a dog in town."

"Yeah," agreed Archer, picturing more mythical headlines. " 'Cocker Kills Mistress. Police Dog Tracks Him Down.' "

"Well, she did at that," said Maclain. "She tipped me off in the diner, Larry—when that fire siren scared her and she shivered against my knee. I remembered petting Winnie at the cocktail party. When the carillon started, he scooted off of the divan. Then at Morse's last night Brownie thought Schnucke was Dreist and was scared to hang around too long." The Captain paused. "I guess he was just plain dumb—not smart at all. Those chimes will be his death knell as well as that of Gallagher and Troy."

"You're pretty damn dumb yourself." Davis gnawed at his badly chewed mustache and winked at Archer.

"I presume," said the Captain, "that you have something on that official tumor which you erroneously refer to as a mind."

"It occurred to me that Archer and I have wives to go home to. We've even united Lucia and Larmar." The inspector gave an elaborate sigh. "Murder is very trying. I thought how nice it would be—now that this death knell has stopped ringing—if you rang a few wedding bells and quit running around with those circus dogs and getting into my eye."

The Captain grinned. "You might tell that to Sybella, Larry." He turned about face in his hospital chair and muttered something that sounded like, "The readiness is all."

(continued from front flap)

spelled disaster for Maclain and his fiancee Sybella as well as:

Larmar Jordan, famous novelist equally successful with varied and sundry women;

Lucia Jordan, his wife, who resented her husband's philanderings but was rather proud of her own;

Troy Singleton, a walking model of a Varga pin-up girl — she "gits thar fustest with the mostest men!"

Paul Hirst, Larmar's secretary whose regard for his employer stopped considerably short of admiration;

Ellis Brown Mitchell, a meticulous little man commonly known as "Brownie," who had a voluminous knowledge of firearms;

Daniel Pine, a wealthy manufacturer of bombers who made a direct hit with Troy;

Winnie, a timid cocker spaniel completely miscast in a role he would never have chosen.

WILLIAM MORROW & COMPANY
425 Fourth Ave.   New York 16

CPSIA information can be obtained
at www.ICGtesting.com
Printed in the USA
BVHW040204081221
623497BV00021B/309